7 Life Lessons Learned Through Loss

Powerful Stories of Love, Hope, Transformation and Legacy

Sharon Muscet

Copyright © Sharon Muscet 2019

Published by Sharon Muscet

ISBN-13: 978-0-6487031-0-5 Paperback

ISBN-13: 978-0-6487031-1-2 EBook

Cover Art by Melissa Pepers, Bonbo

All rights are reserved. No part of this book may be used or reproduced in any form by any electronic, mechanical, or any other device now known or invented hereafter without permission of the author, except in the case of brief quotations embodied in critical articles and reviews. These forms include, but are not limited to xerography, photocopying, scanning, recording, distributing via internet means, information storage and retrieval systems.

Because of the dynamic nature of the internet, any web address or links contained in this book may have changed since publication and may no longer be valid.

Dedication

To my two sons, Luka and Hugo – for showing me the greatest LOVE of all.

You are my world. I want to show you what is possible when you believe in yourself,

and what can happen when you live your life in service to others.

Contents

Introduction vii

Life Lesson 1: Death is LOVE 1

Life Lesson 2: Decide how you want to be remembered .. 35

Life Lesson 3: What it truly means to live your best life 57

Life Lesson 4: Dysfunction in families is normal 97

Life Lesson 5: Be of service to others 129

Life Lesson 6: Be prepared for your death 145

Life Lesson 7: Leave your legacy - record your life story .. 163

Final Words 183

Acknowledgements 189

About the author 197

Introduction

I have always had a fascination with the movie, *The Wizard of Oz*. As a young girl I felt so happy watching this movie. I loved Dorothy for her spark and how she could stand up for herself when she needed to. This girl had a voice. She knew what she wanted. She was kind and respectful to people and animals. She had empathy. Who could forget those ruby red shoes? My Mum said as a young girl, I would always talk about those ruby red shoes and how I wished I could have a pair just like them. I would pretend to click my shoes together three times and say, "*there's no place like home, there's no place like home, there's no place like home.*"

My first memory of *home* and of my childhood was one of freedom. Like Dorothy, I grew up on a farm. For me it was in the country in South Australia. I loved roaming around the paddocks with the chickens, the sheep, and feeding the little lambs. I remember playing hide and seek through the paddock to the side of the house, which was knee high in sour sobs. I would play with my brothers, my sister and neighbours. I would roll over and gaze up at the sky, the clouds and the sun. I felt so free. I called myself *Spirit Girl*.

My mother had the most magnificent rose garden at the front of her house. The roses framed the long front fence. I cannot tell you the number of hours I would spend in that rose garden, smelling each rose on the rose bush. I would start at the first rose bush and make my way along each one – fifteen of them in total – smelling the fragrance of the old-world petals. At the end of the row, I would turn to the right and find the two largest bushes – the peace rose, and the *piece de resistance* – the Queen Elizabeth rose bush. It stood regal and was the tallest of them all. It had the most exquisite fragrance. I believed in fairies and angels and would imagine them to be around me.

Like Dorothy, however, I too became *lost*. One day when I was around eight years old, my childhood memory of freedom was shattered, with an incident which was to impact my life. I felt frightened and unsure what to do. After the incident, I ran and sat right beside the Queen Elizabeth rose bush, as if she were my protector. I crouched down for what seemed like an eternity.

What was going through my mind besides shock, was what to do next. It was a sliding door moment. My twin brother had run around looking for me, saying, *"There you are. What are you doing?"* Then asking, *"What's wrong?"* I put on a fake smile and said, *"Nothing."* I chose silence over truth.

I changed from that day forward. I remember my father saying that as a child, sometimes I was like this little scared rabbit. I recall I had become untrusting of people. I had lost confidence within myself, I lost my voice. I had self-doubt. *Spirit Girl* was gone. I no longer felt *home*.

From that time on, the only thing that gave me a sense of freedom, was running. I loved that feeling of being completely free. I used to love running in the sports days, and any race meets.

I hadn't noticed until that time, of the limiting self-belief I had. When I found I wasn't running as fast as I used to, all doubt crept in. I would torment myself with words of self-doubt.

One day we had our Annual Sports Day. I vividly recall

walking to the race meet with the negative self-talk in my head saying, "*You won't win; you aren't fast; you will embarrass yourself.*" The words went over and over in my head. That is when I heard it. A voice that changed everything.

It was a man's loud booming voice in my ear, over my right shoulder. He must have heard the negative self-talk I was saying. His voice boomed, "*SHARON, BELIEVE.*" I swung my head around so fast, to see who was there. There was no-one. It was like an electrical charge had gone through my body. I was scared, yet, exhilarated at the same time.

I can't tell you who or what that voice was. What I can tell you though is that my self-doubt and negative self-talk simply vanished. I said to myself, "*Sharon, believe. Sharon, believe. Sharon, believe. You are the strongest. You are the fittest. You are the tallest. You can win this.*"

I said these words over and over again. As I went to take my mark for the 100-metre race – a race I hadn't won for quite some time now - I said it over and over, "*Sharon, believe.*" The gun went off and as I ran, I said the words over and over again. Guess what? I won!

I was so excited that I signed myself up for the 200

and 400-metre race, winning both. I couldn't believe it. At this young age I remember saying to myself, "*WOW! I have THE SECRET – if I put my mind to something, and believe it, if I do the work, then I can make anything happen!*"

From that day on, something inside me changed. At the age of twelve, I realised the magnitude of believing in myself. I started to apply it to many things. I believed I would get picked for the volleyball squad, and I did. I believed I would get picked for the SAPSASA netball side, and I did. I believed the cutest boy in class would ask me out, and he did!

Two years later, I left the country farm and moved to Adelaide to attend Boarding School. I arrived at the start of Year 11. It was like this whole new world opened up for me with new opportunities, new friendships; a new life.

In Year 12, one of my teachers said to me, "*Sharon you have what it takes to top the State in Legal Studies. I believe in you. I will mentor you.*" That was the first time I ever recall anyone saying that THEY believed in me. This in turn had my own belief in me grow ten-fold. I put in the hard work for one whole year. I believed that I would top the State. Guess what? I did! The concept of belief had again worked for me.

What I knew was that if I truly believed in something, and took action and worked hard, the results would come. I would not allow for self-doubt to creep in.

Life was good. I had attended University and obtained my Bachelor of Education, majoring in Business and I first went into the realm of Adult Education and Training. Following this I became a Training Manager with a large Law firm. I continued to work my way up the corporate ladder, and at the age of thirty three, I found myself working on the other side of the world as a PR and Marketing Executive for a world-wide company. I was based in their United Kingdom office and each week I would travel extensively throughout Europe. I had signed a three year contract. It was a senior role with opportunities to further climb the corporate ladder in other countries around the world. I was so excited to have been given this promotion. I was at the time a self-confessed workaholic. I was single and completely dedicated to my role. It offered exciting opportunities to travel the world and meet amazing people. I was happy to work overseas, earning an incredible income, and set myself up for my future financially. But, the

Universe had other plans. I was about to be tested.

I recall four weeks after arriving in London, on a Sunday — and Sundays were my most homesick days — walking around the shops in King Street, Hyde Park. I was in a shop, trying on hats. I recall feeling sad. I distinctly recall asking this question to myself, *"How long am I going to be here?"* when I heard a loud, booming voice yell back at me over my right shoulder, *"SIX MONTHS."*

I turned my head to see who the man was who had just yelled at me. There was no one there. I instinctively knew it was that same voice I had first heard when I was twelve years old. I have always felt this voice was my *Guide*. I answered him back, out loud I might add, saying, *"Well that can't be true, I have signed a contract for three years."*

In my employment contract, it had stated if I was to break my contract within three years, I owed the company, understandably, a substantial amount of money in relocation costs and other expenses, so for me, breaking contract was never an option. So, I dismissed this guidance instantly and didn't think about it again for some time.

This is where my story gets interesting. It was at this time, many things started to go wrong for me. Shortly after this day, my drink was spiked with a terrible illicit drug, thankfully my friends were there to help me. It was a frightening experience. My car was broken into and my mobile phone stolen. I was abused by a taxi driver where I literally jumped from his travelling taxi. I travelled over to Ireland on one occasion on a work trip, when suddenly I was unable to see. Just like that I couldn't open my eyes.

I couldn't understand why suddenly things were starting to go wrong for me. I recalled those words of Dorothy - *there's no place like home, there's no place like home, there's no place like home* - going over and over in my head. I really wanted to go home. It seems the Universe was conspiring to make it happen.

After three weeks, I travelled back to Australia on a work trip with twenty of our top distributors from around the world. My boss, my colleague and I were to be *working* for the next two weeks. We had just arrived at our hotel room, our only afternoon off for the next two weeks, when I decided to go for a swim at one of our beautiful Adelaide beaches. I was paddling in the water when I had a freak accident.

This accident was to change my life forever. I stepped

on the tail of a sting-ray.

Cast your mind back to Steve Irwin, the famous Australian Crocodile Hunter. He had an encounter where the barb from a sting-ray went through his heart and cost him his life. His encounter happened two years after mine.

The result of the sting-ray barb going through the bottom of my foot was horrendous. I spent the next two years in and out of hospital, in a wheelchair and with a PICC line attached to my arm. I had ten operations and on two occasions was fighting to save the toes on my left foot from amputation. On another two occasions I nearly lost my life. I looked death straight in the eye. The toxins that ravaged through my body played havoc with me, as did the antibiotics permanently pumped through my body. My liver was badly affected and, for a time, turned the whites of my eyes orange. I was in despair. These were some of the toughest days of my life. I was also told I would never run again. This broke my heart.

I was forced to return to Australia to convalesce with family and friends. My home was being rented out, so I was homeless and living on friends' couches in between hospital stays. After twelve months I had to make the difficult decision to relinquish my role with the company. I was left with a permanent partial disability of my left foot. It is filled with plates and screws and I have neuropathy, meaning I have lost feeling in my left foot.

This accident changed me and my life completely. Upon reflection, I can now say that this accident was the best thing that ever happened to me. I believe that homesick feeling that I had so strongly since the time I arrived into London, was my deep intuition that I was not where I was meant to be.

Two years is a very long time to be off your feet. Always one to see the positive, I decided to devote myself to the things I had always wanted to do. I thought there is something happening here – I am being prepared for something bigger and better than I have ever thought possible. I believed that I had to, there was no other option or explanation. I refused to play a victim.

I saw it that the Universe was already looking after me – for those two years I was still paid a full-time income with income protection by my employer, plus my rent was being paid. I had a company car and they paid my mobile phone even though I wasn't able to work for them. I felt incredibly fortunate at this time, despite the condition of my health.

Knowing I was somehow being looked after, I decided to dedicate my time to doing the things I loved or had always wanted to do. I knew I had to keep my spirits up, to stay as positive as I could during one of the most difficult times of my life. First thing was to take up singing lessons. Singing is something I had always wanted to do. It made me so happy and I looked forward to every week having these classes. It literally made my heart sing. I took up knitting as I had always wanted to knit myself a scarf. I found this incredibly meditative. I took up mosaic classes and immersed myself in the creative process of mosaics and made many things for myself. I studied to become a marriage celebrant – something I had always wanted to do. I delved further into meditation and began teaching meditation classes to others. I learnt about Numerology and began to complete Numerology charts for people. I became qualified at Reiki and Energy Healing. I opened up a Healing practice and had weekly clients who would come to see me.

It's interesting what actually started happening – through being of service to other people and helping others, it was aiding in my own healing. It was during this time, I had starting dating a man who had actually been a good friend for eighteen months prior to my accident. We had met prior to me living overseas. During the time of my accident he had been a wonderful friend. One thing led to another and we got together and after ten months of dating we were married. Twelve months after that our first child Luka was born, and sixteen months later, our second son Hugo was born.

Things were beginning to feel *home* for me. Despite my ongoing challenges with my physical health and ongoing operations on my foot (my healing took six years in total), I was in a very good place spiritually, emotionally and mentally. I was a Mum now. Something I never thought I would be. I was so happy. They were my little miracles. My life took on a whole new meaning.

Once the boys were two and three years old and my health was back on track, I started up my own network marketing business with a global brand. My accident had set me back literally hundreds and thousands of dollars in lost earnings. So, with my power to believe, I got to work, not only for me but for my husband and children as well.

It was shortly after this time, however, that another tragedy for me hit when I had a heart attack. I stared death in the face again. That day I fought for my life. I wasn't ready to go. I have my boys now. I still have so much life to live. It was several days after this happened, when this overwhelming sense of peace washed over me. I thought - *If I was meant to be gone, I'd be gone. But I'm not, I'm here. I'm here for a reason.*

I once heard someone say what happens to you in life is no accident. Each little piece that happens in your life is like a jigsaw piece. You piece it all together, bit by bit, to create something extraordinary. That is what I believe has happened. Piece by piece like the jigsaw, it was actually all coming together. Every little experience was building upon the next and the next, to create a life that was truly magical. Despite all of my obstacles, I continued to believe there was something incredible awaiting me. I wasn't sure what, but I had faith. It's a bit like Dorothy, all the time she was lost, she always believed she would find Oz.

Shortly after this time, my best friend's father passed away. She asked me to conduct his entire funeral service. I had celebrancy experience having studied to be a marriage celebrant and conducted several weddings, but I had never conducted a funeral before.

I was nervous when my friend asked me, however it was for her, her family and her father, so I did it. That day changed my life. Being able to be there for all of them, at one of the saddest times in their life and deliver a beautiful service that they will remember, was so rewarding for me. I recall driving home thinking - *It just feels right. I cannot describe it, I know I am where I am meant to be*. It was the moment I realised I had just *lived on purpose*. It was the most incredible moment when I realised this. I have been living on purpose ever since.

That was in 2011. Since then I have conducted several hundred *Celebrations of Life* for those who have passed, ranging from the age of a baby at thirty two week's gestation, right up until the age of one hundred and two years old. All are unique. This is the most rewarding work and I am proud to say I have found my calling.

It is a privilege to work with families whilst grieving, to create a moving and fitting ceremony for their loved one. However, it is not just about meeting with families, writing a service and delivering a service. To me it is so much more.

I believe I have been sent to these families for a reason. I am not just there to deliver the service. I am there to send light and love, peace and healing to all who are there in the chapel, including myself.

I have such an unshakeable belief in what I do. From the day I undertook my first service, I knew I had found my calling and was here for a purpose. When I work with a family, let's say a family has just lost their child. It is unfathomable what the family goes through. It is incredibly emotional and difficult. I feel if I can make just a small difference to this family at the most difficult time in their life, by honouring their child in a beautiful way and having them focus on the love, then I have been of service to them. I have no feelings to describe that. The work I do comes from a place in my heart, of deep love and connection.

I see it as my purpose to impact every single person who is there. To help them through their grieving process. Through my writing and my words, I strive to bring to life the meaning and purpose of the departed. Life for me again, felt amazing as I was being of service, I could see everything that had happened up until this point, was all for a reason.

It is in my experiences of working with these families and hearing their loved one's life stories, that I realised every single life has a meaning and a purpose. We all have an incredible story to share. We all have life lessons within us that we can share with others, hence the writing of this book. My aim is to share powerful stories, life lessons and love stories from those who have passed with a view to helping others live their best life.

My work is such a privilege. I sit with a family and I hear their most personal feelings about LOVE, when their loved one passes. I hear the most incredible love stories. I see the love a parent has for their child and a child has for their parent. I hear stories of dysfunction, torn apart by love. Yes, I see hearts breaking in front of me, every day, but it's born out of love. Through this work, I have learned the most incredible life lessons. I now see it as my purpose to share these lessons with the world. Dr Wayne Dyer's famous quote says, "*When we change the way we look at things, the things we look at change.*" Death is LOVE.

I am the Founder of *The Love in Death* movement which is the coming together of people from all around the world who share two things in common – they have all loved someone, and they have lost their loved one through death.

The Love in Death movement is literally changing the way we view death by shifting society's focus from fear, to one of love, through focusing on love stories and the incredible life lessons that can be learned.

The Love in Death movement is so much bigger than me. I am merely the messenger – delivering a very important message worldwide. This is my life's purpose. I have found *home*.

Today, I am called upon as a celebrated international keynote speaker, to share powerful stories, life lessons and love stories from those who have passed with a view of helping others live their best life. Inspiring audiences all over the world to reflect on their own life, to transform them to take action and change not only the way they die but the way in which they live their life.

I had this amazing fantasy about my life, from a very little girl, about how it would look. My life has looked nothing like that at all. However, from the actions that changed the course of my life, something incredible came of it – the concept of BELIEVE.

I have taught my two boys the concept of *believe* with incredible results, so much so that their school invited me to share with other children. Now it is my passion to teach that self-belief to others.

In writing this book, it is my intention to be a No. 1 best-selling author – stay tuned for that one. I believe in it, so it will happen!

I also had a fascination with Glinda, the Good Witch of the South, in the Wizard of Oz. Glinda was a White Witch and from the time she magically appeared across the screen in her bubble, I was entranced. She was so beautiful. Wearing her almighty crown – so regal. Her beautiful sparkling dress – one might say a little over the top, but her white, sequined dress was the most beautiful I had ever seen. She was so beautiful and so kind to Dorothy and all of the little Munchkins in Munchkin land. She was their protector. She had magical powers. She was the one who gave the rights of those ruby red shoes to Dorothy and told her to follow the yellow brick road all the way to Oz where she would be able to meet the great Wizard of Oz who will transport her home. She poured belief into Dorothy that this was in fact, her way home.

I was captivated by her mystery, her magic, her power. She was so kind, had such presence. She was so certain. She showed no fear, not even to the Wicked Witch of the West who terrified me. I had come to realise that I too have the powers of Glinda. We all do.

In the final scenes of the movie, she flew in, inside her bubble, to the balcony where Dorothy and the Wizard of Oz stood. She spoke the most magical words I have ever heard. Still to this day they are the words that I hold most dear to me. She said, *"You had the power all along, My Dear. All you had to do was believe it for yourself."* And with three clicks of those ruby red shoes Dorothy was home. Dorothy had that power all along to get home. All she had to do was believe in herself and her own abilities. No one else could do it for her. No Wizard and no White Witch. It was her belief in herself to create anything that her heart truly desired.

We are all born with a power inside us that is extraordinary. We all possess the power to achieve incredible things, despite what life throws our way. It's whether we believe it, that sets us apart from others.

I believe in the power to believe. *Do you?*

Life Lesson 1:

Death is LOVE

Sharon Muscet

7 Life Lessons Learned Through Loss

Have you ever noticed there is so much fear that surrounds death? In Western society, it is seen as this *taboo topic* and we are so uncomfortable talking about it. Why is that? Death is a natural part of life; as natural as birth. We have all been affected by death in some way – the death of a loved one or even a brush with death ourselves. What emotions arise for you when you think of death? Sit with that for a moment and feel how it feels for you.

I acknowledge there are different religions and they have differing opinions on death and even the after-life. I acknowledge them all. I am not here to judge nor do I wish judgment to be placed upon me. What I wish to share with you are my learnings being in this line of work. I have no religious agenda to any of my thoughts. These are my own learnings from the thousands of individuals I have worked alongside experiencing the realities of death. This has given me a privileged insight into not only how to cope with grief and loss, but more importantly, the life lessons learned from those who pass.

Many people see death as final; it is dark, and it is the end. It is incredibly sad. It is fearful. In fact, it is the actual process – the *how* - of dying that many people fear. It is the longing and missing a person after they have died. What I have discovered through my work about death, is that it's all about LOVE. I see love in its finest form. I do not work in the death industry, I see it that I am in the industry of love.

I sit with a family and I hear their most personal thoughts about love when their loved one passes. It is such a privilege. I hear the most incredible love stories. I see the love a child has for their parent when their parent passes. I see the love a parent has for their child when their child passes. I see the love a parent has for their unborn child. Yes, I see hearts breaking every day, but it's all borne out of love. I hear stories and see dysfunction in families. I hear and see the absolute devastation at the loss of life. This devastation and this grief are all borne out of love. You see, death IS love. Without this love, you cannot have grief. Grief is the unspent love you have for a person. It's the tears in your eyes, it's the pain in your heart. Whenever we are grieving the loss of our loved one, we are *loving* the loss of our loved one. We are pouring out our love that we have for them. We shed tears of *love*.

Rather than think about death as final, it's changing the

way we see it. Death is love in its purest form. The death of a person may change a relationship, but it does not end it. Even after death, you may still continue a relationship with your loved one. It is still personal, real and just as meaningful. Nothing can ever take away from the special time that you shared with this person. Nothing can ever take away from the love that they had for you, or you had for them. The love that was there is still there, and will be there forever more.

We have created illusions surrounding death. That it is final. Everything stops. There is no doubt that the relationship does certainly change through death, as our loved ones are no longer physically with us. However, the bond of love transcends death.

We are all born into LOVE. We leave this world in LOVE. As Deepak Copra suggests, *"Love is the most powerful force in the Universe; it can heal and inspire."* What goes on in between is up to us. I believe when we see a young baby and they smile, they are seeing love in its truest form. Have you noticed how much children laugh with not a care in the world? They see pure love.

As we get older, something starts to happen – we start

to become influenced by people, by judgments; sometimes the harsh realities of life can hit us. Greed, ego, selfishness and want comes into play. We move further and further away from our true self, from that true love we were born into. There are temptations at every turn. We can no longer see in the path of love or what has been laid before us. Instead, we take some winding road, dodging and weaving until sometimes we can see no further and we cannot see a way out.

It is said by palliative nurses who care for the sick, that in the days leading up to their passing, is when they witness peace, forgiveness, pure joy and pure love. Why is that? I believe leading up to their passing, as their body starts to slow down, their mind starts to slow down too. Instead of remembering the material things that were once important to them, their heart starts to fill up with love.

They are being led back to pure love. The road starts to become clear for them and they start to see what it is that was intended for them. Their purpose in life. They start to see that the small things in life are actually the most important things. Family, love, joy and peace is what true life is all about. Our task in this lifetime is to find true peace, true joy, true love, true light. It is to be of service to others. By being of true service to others, we come to find true love in our hearts.

When we are led back to love, our journey in life becomes clear and our reason for living becomes clear. We start to feel *no fear*. Death is nothing to be feared. Death is just a word. It surprises me how many people fear death, yet when you think about it, what is it that people truly fear? Is it you fear how you will die? Where you go? What happens to you? What will happen to your family? Will you ever see your family again?

When you die it is not that you feel nothing; your death is when you feel the purest form of love, you feel a peace and a love like no other. It is just like when you are born into this world, you feel true love and true peace.

Grief is the unspent love. There is no doubt that the death of a loved one leaves one feeling grief stricken. In my experience there are many different forms of grief. The grief I see for a child who has passed is different to the grief when it is a suicide. It is much different again to the grief when it has been a sudden death like a car accident, or the grief for a person who has died from a terminal illness.

Then there is grief after someone passed in their sleep of old age.

Describing grief can be difficult. It was this explanation from a granddaughter at her grandfather's funeral that best explained it for me. She had lost her grandmother four weeks earlier. The gentleman and his wife had been married for forty-four years. The family believe the pain of him being apart from his wife was too great and he passed on four weeks after her.

I had read a tribute on behalf of the granddaughter at his *Celebration of Life* and her paragraph on grief took my breath away.

"At moments I catch myself feeling selfish to be so sad that you are now gone, like really gone. It really hurts and everyone talks about grief, but after so much loss in such a short time, I don't believe in grief, per say, I just believe in love. Grief is just the unspent love that builds up and hurts, because it has nowhere to go anymore. All the things we wish we could have said or done, it piles in the corners of our eyes and lumps in our throats and just really hurts...."

7 Life Lessons Learned Through Loss

In my experience as someone who sees and deals with grief on a daily basis, I am here to tell you that the biggest fear is the family not knowing where their loved one has gone. This is what can hold them back from moving on. The fear of not knowing - *are they okay?* - is the question that they ask the most.

I am here to tell you my story about my own personal experience with death. You see, I believe I have seen heaven. I have seen where we go. I am here to tell you that what I have seen and what I felt was a love purer than we have experienced on this earth.

I was in my late thirties. It was during this time that I was working with my spiritual counsellor. As my own guidance and intuition was growing, I had the most incredible experience. I have been one of the very few blessed in this world to see what happens when one passes. I feel I have witnessed pure love and pure joy before my own passing.

I have never experienced a love like it. I was blessed to have helped a man who had passed, cross over into the after-life. A frightened man, too scared and caught in-between. I watched whilst he was called upon by the most extraordinary love. There was indeed a tunnel to walk along and at the end was a person, holding out his hand and waiting to join him. I could hear the sweetest sounds in their purest form. It was peace like I have never experienced before. It was love like I have never experienced before. Time stood still. Tears of pure love slipped down my face, from my eyes. In its purest form. As I watched this man walk into the tunnel, a man reached out taking his hand and together they walked into the light.

After this experience occurred, I looked around me. The sounds were sweeter, the colours were much more vivid, it seemed like there was no time; It was different. Everything was altered for me. I had been of true service and now life was so different for me.

It is a love that is indescribable. It is a love that I am so honoured to have witnessed and to have felt. It is a love that we all will return to one day. Since then I have never been afraid of dying or death or where we go. Therefore, it is my firm belief, there is nothing to fear. Your loved one is in an incredible place. I have also heard of many near death experiences as well, and they have all described this same feeling of love and peace. It is not like earth. It is a space where only pure love is felt.

If you have experienced the passing of a loved one, I believe they are in pure love. If you are fearful of your own passing, I believe that you will go to a place of pure love and peace. Where time stands still. There are other loved ones waiting to meet you in the form of spirit. The moment they walk towards the great white light, they are surrounded in that love, to fulfil their soul's next journey. It is like they are in the next room. You cannot see them but they can hear you. In your heart you will feel them. You will feel them speaking to you. Know they are all around you, showering you with love.

Learning from the young – there is no fear in death, only LOVE

"Every single free choice you make, arises from either a thought of love or a thought of fear.
There is no other choice."
Neale Donald Walshe, 'Conversations with God.'

By far, the most challenging part of my role as a Funeral Celebrant is conducting a service for a baby or a young child, taken far too soon. The grief encountered by the families is like no other. How does a parent say goodbye to their child? It doesn't matter what age their child is – a baby, a young child, or an adult. The grief is always the same. A parent's grief is indescribable. I literally see hearts breaking right before my eyes.

When the elderly depart we recognise a natural change. It kind of feels normal – the end of a lifetime and life span encompassing all that was to be given and achieved. The passing of a young child seems so unfair, so needless, a waste of a life that had so much to give.

As a mother of two boys, I cannot help but feel what these families are feeling. As a Funeral Celebrant, this is when I need to be at my strongest.

The first service I ever conducted for a child, was for a young girl, Isabella, aged 6 years. The sadness I witnessed this day was indescribable. Many times during the service I had to stop myself from crying. Yet, the Funeral Director, whom I have done so many services with since, said this service was outstanding. The best she had seen me do. How did I do it? I often ask myself that question. My only explanation was wanting to be of service for the family and to honour their beloved child. Driving home, I burst into tears. I held my sadness in until I was no longer needed by the family. However, I am human and there is no way you can get through something like that without truly feeling it and having it affect you.

I strive to help the family find a meaning and purpose of their child's life and turn it into a story to share on the day. It is one way of honouring their child's life. On this day, the story that I delivered at Isabella's service was one of love, courage, faith and hope.

An adaptation of her story is as follows:

"LOVE - Isabella only knew pure love. The love she shared with her mother was incredible. They were best friends who had an incredible bond. Her mother shared that all her life she wished for a beautiful girl, with strawberry blonde hair and blue eyes. She must have wished for it enough, as her beautiful baby girl with strawberry blonde hair and blue eyes was born. She was known by many nicknames – Issy, Monkey and Rabbit Nose, but it was the name – Isabella - that Isabella liked and she told people to call her that. It was much more grown up.

Isabella was loved by all of her family. A highlight of

their life together was when Make a Wish Foundation granted her wish and flew the family to the snow for seven days. She absolutely loved this time with her family. She took lessons for tobogganing, she went tubing, she made snow angels and snow men. It was a wish come true for her and she just loved it.

Isabella loved many other things including gummy bears, Ninja Turtles and Spiderman. She loved dressing up for Halloween. She loved her Play Station. She loved running around with the other kids. She loved music and would watch music videos for days on end. She loved that she got to be the poster child for many different things, including the SA Health Website, twice. Her personality was infectious to those around her.

She was a loving, cheeky, mischievous girl. A girl who loved the colour red. Red is the colour of passion and love. It needs no explanation therefore as to why she would love it so much. Isabella in her six years only knew true love. To her family, you have shown Isabella more love than some people would feel in a lifetime. She was born into love, lived this life surrounded by love, she still feels your love, and she is now surrounded by love in another place.

7 Life Lessons Learned Through Loss

COURAGE – I think of Isabella and of her courage throughout her life. She was a fighter, of that there is no doubt. She was diagnosed with Leukaemia almost one year before her passing, and underwent so much. Something no person should ever have to endure. Yet she took it all in her stride. Her mother told me it didn't bother her. She would tell the nurses what to do! She was always inquisitive, wanting to know what they were doing. She only ever got to attend her first six months at school and made many friends and loved being around the other kids. When she became unwell and her treatment in hospital started she had hospital school teachers that would do lessons with her. She was so adaptable to anything that came her way.

Isabella was very strong, even when she was in pain she wouldn't take anything for it. She was a fighter and she fought a hard battle. When her hair had to be shaved, rather than be sad, she took it all in her stride and started wearing her gangster-flat brimmed hat which she absolutely loved. She never saw the bad in anything, only wonderful new exiting opportunities. When it was decided she would have no more treatment, this little girl just listened, and didn't ask any questions. She was the bravest girl I have ever known.

There is no doubt that she showed tremendous courage in adversity and sadly, yet courageously, at the age of six years, with her beautiful mother by her side, it was time for Isabella to leave this world.

FAITH – Hearing how Isabella accepted her condition, and asked no questions, shows me that this little girl had so much faith. She had faith in her mother, faith in her doctors, her nurses, her play therapist, her friends, and her family. She had faith in her life. She had faith that when she was told there was nothing more that could be done for her, she took it in her stride, as she had done all her life – and surrendered to it. She left this world in love. She wasn't afraid or scared. She just accepted it.

I think all of us can learn so much from this beautiful little girl with her strawberry blonde hair and blue eyes. Isabella was a dreamer. Despite her illness she had many dreams – one was to go to the snow. She had a dream to swim with the dolphins, she had a dream to go horse riding. She had many career options – one was to win a medal gold at the Olympic Games as a diver. She was also to become a ballerina, a doctor, a nurse and a play therapist. Isabella dreamed big and there was nothing that would stop her dreaming big.

From that, we can learn a great lesson in faith. Even in adversity she continued to be positive, to dream big, to live, to fight. She had faith that what would be, would be. We can all learn so many lessons from that and hold great faith in knowing she is now in a place filled with love, looking down on all of you, and still leaving her mark on this world.

HOPE – it is her mother's hope for you all that we all learn something from Isabella's passing. This is a profound loss, there is no doubt. Isabella has taught us all the importance of life. To savour every single moment you have with a loved one. Isabella's passing has caused us all to take pause and truly value the things most important to us in life, to live life fully, to dream big, to never ever take anything for granted, and most of all to love. Life is far too precious. Isabella is a true gift and a miracle."

I have conducted many services for young children. What astounds me with each story the family share with me, is the bravery and acceptance of these little people. They show no fear around death. They live life to the full and accept their situation. They do not fear where they are going. They live in the present and fully feel the love they are surrounded by in this life. What an incredible privilege to learn from these beautiful little people. They have certainly left their mark on this world.

It certainly doesn't take away from the sadness of these little people losing their lives and I have no doubt there is still a huge void in the heart of their loved ones and they would still ask the question of *why* every day. My heart goes out to each and every family who have ever encountered this.

I think it is like what I have already said: As we get older, something starts to happen. We move further and further away from our true self, from that true love and from our true guidance. We can no longer see the path of love, of what has been laid before us. Yet in these instances for young children, they still see love, only love.

Death IS love. There is nothing to fear. I call it – *The Love in Death*.

My work is an incredible privilege. Each day, I witness love in its purest form. People stand before me and share their most personal feelings about love, when their loved one passes. It is the greatest gift for me to hear that. Whether it be the love of a parent and a child, love of a child to a parent, love of a husband and a wife, the love of a family member, love of a friend, love of a work colleague, love of an ex-partner. I see it all. I hear it all. We are born into love and we leave in love, but what happens in between is up to us. Do you choose to live a life full of love or otherwise?

The Love in Death: Love Stories of Loss

I hear the most beautiful stories about love. I wish to share the following stories with you. I share it to inspire you, to live your best life, by surrounding yourself in that love. I share it so you too can discover *The Love in Death*.

I hear so many stories about love at first sight, I hear stories of how hearts were broken by love, and then rebuilt on love. I hear stories of unconditional love. I hear of complete and utter heartbreak of a love for a baby that the parents had not yet met. I hear of long-lasting love. I hear of husbands or wives who have spent 50, 60, 70 years together, die very shortly after their loved one has departed because of their broken heart. I see people write and deliver the most heart-wrenching tributes of their loved ones, of what they meant to them. I see people who have gone through the cruellest of circumstances, still be filled with so much love. They are often the ones with so much to give. I see those that have the simplest of lives, yet, they have so much love to give.

I sit and listen in awe of these people. I hope these following stories inspire you. I hope they allow you to sit back and reflect on the love that you surround yourself with daily. I hope they allow you to see that we are all love, and all you need in life is love.

I once came from a funeral service where I felt absolutely overwhelmed with love. A guest said to me as I was leaving, *"you must have one of the hardest jobs in the world."* I replied to him, *"I have one of the most rewarding jobs in the world. I get to meet and speak with incredible families and hear love stories of their loved ones who have passed."*

I hear many stories of love at first sight. Whilst the story is different in how people meet, it is always the same. It is the first glance that took their breath away. Some of these people who tell me their love stories are well into their nineties now, yet they tell it with a sparkle in their eye and reminisce like it was only yesterday. I have always been intrigued by this. How can it be that when two people meet, they can simply fall in love? What is it that ignites between them? How do they *know* they have found *the one* after simply meeting them? How then do they turn it into a lifelong love?

I am a true romantic and love a good love story, so it is such a privilege that I share in these stories with them, at such a difficult time, when they are saying goodbye to their greatest love. Their stories give me hope.

I had led a *Celebration of Life* for a man named Les, who was ninety four years old when he passed. His wife for seventy years, Phyllis, was there to say goodbye to him. She had told me when they first met at a dance, their eyes glanced from across the room and that was it for them. They fell in love. He had asked a friend, *"who is that?"* and was swiftly introduced to her. That night he drove her home on his motorbike and she was smitten. They were married not a year later, and it was to be eight years until they started their family. They raised two children and endured the pain of losing one of them when he was just seventeen years old.

Sharon Muscet

Every day, even up until his final days of his ninety four years, he would hold his wife's hand and say, *"the love of my life, the love of my life,"* over and over again. They were always holding hands and touching. They led a very social life with lots of friends, card games and parties. They travelled all over Australia. They were true companions and inseparable.

I asked her, *"so what is the secret to your long and happy marriage?"* I expected some long, deep and meaningful answer. She just shrugged her shoulders and said, *"I married my best friend,"* as if to say isn't that what everyone does?

I first met Phyllis a few days after her husband's passing. She was sad, yet quite chipper, sitting up in her chair at the nursing home, recalling many wonderful stories of her time with Les. There were no tears shed, only good memories. However, at the service I conducted for them one week later, I saw a very different composure. The shock of losing the love of her life had well and truly set in. Unable to walk, she was brought into the chapel in a wheelchair. She looked so frail in the week since I had seen her. She was in tears, shedding many tears of love. Phyllis was missing him terribly. She was taken to his coffin and I watched as she placed her hand on it, she looked straight at it, in silence.

What was going through her mind? How could you contain that type of love? Where would you even start? She was shattered. It broke my heart to see her like that. All I can do is offer her comfort at this time and lead a wonderful celebration of her husband's life. I shared their love story with those that had attended the service. It was nice to see a smile break over Phyllis's face as she reflected on and remembered their love for one another - the love in death.

Often my heart is secretly breaking for them as they say their last goodbyes. It is surreal for me as I watch that. I cannot help but wonder how I would feel if that were me, saying goodbye, to the love of my life. I watch them at the coffin. I am not watching to pry, I am watching them to ensure their health and wellbeing is okay. Often these people are frail themselves and the stress of their breaking heart is too much for them to bear.

Days like that are tough for me to see, yet, I am grateful to see the heartbreak, for without that I would not see true love. I am sure whilst these families' hearts are breaking, they would not have any regrets and do it all again in a heartbeat, because they found true love and they experienced many years with their one true love. Some people can go through a whole lifetime and never experience true love nor ever experience love at first sight.

Another beautiful story that comes to my mind of love at first sight, was of a lady named Claire who had passed aged ninety two years old. I had actually met her six months prior when I was the Celebrant who conducted the *Celebration of Life* for her daughter. It is always a great privilege when a family request me to come back and conduct other family members' services. Her husband, Graham, always managed to see the positive in any situation and he looked at his wife's passing as feeling so grateful for the sixty four years he had with her.

He shared with me that when they met, it was love at first sight. Graham mentioned he had met her at a dance two years prior to their marriage. He saw her and straight away commented to his friend that he liked the way she was dancing and what she was wearing. Before he knew it, however, she had disappeared. It was a few months later when he attended another dance and Claire walked in. He plucked up the courage to speak to her and said, *"I've seen you somewhere before."* She replied with, *"I've heard that five hundred times!"* He told her every detail of what she had been wearing the first time he saw her. She was shocked. During the interval, he talked to her over a milkshake, with two straws, and walked her back to the nurses' quarters after the dance. It was three weeks before he was to see her again, and the rest they say is history.

Again, it was this glancing across the room, this spark that ignited. This force that couldn't keep them apart. I found myself wondering what happened in those three weeks prior to them seeing one another again? Did they pine for each other? What were their thoughts? Is it absence makes the heart grow fonder? In those days there were no mobile phones or even telephones for them to contact one another, they relied on telegrams in the mail. It is all too easy these days to send a quick text message or arrange a time to meet. We live in a very different world. Yet despite our differences in the years and with technology and communication, when love shows up, love shows up. There is no stopping it.

Sharon Muscet

Is it fate that drives people together? Is it destiny? Is it luck? Was it luck Graham attended the second dance again meeting Claire? Was it luck that Phyllis and Les attended that first dance together? I think not, I think it was fate and destiny who came knocking.

I am always fascinated by people's stories of when two people fall in love. From my observations with these families, while there is an instant connection and love at first sight, it is the communication, the understanding, the devotion, the loyalty, the hard work, the forgiveness, the physical touch, that keeps this love going strong. It is a commitment that takes a life time to fulfil. My life is all the richer for having heard these stories. Without Death there is no Love, right? It is *The Love in Death*.

I delivered a service for a woman in her sixties named Liz, who fought cancer for the last seven years. She put up the toughest battle. She was loved and she loved so many people. She had an extraordinary story. Her husband delivered her eulogy. He met his wife and instantly he fell in love with her and within forty-eight hours he knew he wanted to marry her. Within three and a half weeks they were married and their marriage spanned thirty-five years prior to her passing.

She had three boys, two boys prior to them meeting so I could really relate to them, being a mother of two boys myself. He then adopted them and together they had their third child which, he explained to me, tied the whole family together. The husband, the three sons and their eldest grandchild all spoke about her and I was absolutely overwhelmed with how much love they had for her.

I have met with hundreds and hundreds of families, and this family overwhelmed me. She loved butterflies so her daughter-in-law made hand-made butterflies for everyone to wear, including me. She loved the colour red, she wore it every day, so we all wore red. She loved red roses so there were red roses everywhere. We celebrated her and celebrated her life.

Her favourite song was *The Rose,* which was written by Amanda McBroom and was then made famous by Bette Midler who recorded it. This song and the words were a favourite of Liz's and the family asked me to read the lyrics during the service. I had looked up the meaning of this song and explained to the congregation this song is not necessarily one about romantic love. Rather, it is a song on how one should approach and live life. There was a lesson to learn from this song. Only *you* can determine whether or not there will be love in your life. That is what she means when she says, "*I say love, it is a flower ... and you ... it's only seed.*" Only *you* have the power to fill your world with love.

In this case, Liz really did live her life by this. She filled her world with true love in her life. In return, in her time of passing, she was surrounded by the most amazing love. True love at its finest. Liz fought for seven years for her life, for her children and her husband and she underwent so much for them, because she loved them so much and wanted to be with them for as long as she could. I came away very emotional, it took everything in me not to break down and cry during the service. I walked away feeling so honoured.

Be open to love, love and receive love. At the end of the day, that's what life is about. It is about being of service to other people and that is why I do what I do. I know I made a difference in the life of this family. They were overjoyed with the service and I couldn't ask for more.

The lesson is, it doesn't matter about material things, it

doesn't matter about how much money you have, what you do, or where you live. At the end of the day, it comes down to how much you were open to love, how much you loved, and how much love you receive in the world.

Another lady who comes to mind was ninety-one when she passed. Her name was Beth. When I met with the family there was over ten people in that room. Her husband had passed away and they had been married for thirty-six years before his passing. I am told they were completely devoted to one another and were each other's one and only.

Beth lived for her family – in fact I am told her life was all about her family and caring for other people. She was a loved mother, an adored Nana to six, and a cherished Great-Nana to seven. Her family was everything to her and I am told she relinquished a lot of her own life to dedicate that to her family.

She was loved by everyone and she saw the good in everyone around her. She never judged. She was adored by so many people. That was clearly evident to me. She was still caring about other people right up until the day she passed. She was like a second mother to her three grandchildren. She was known as *Nan* to everyone who came into contact with her - her grandchildren, great-grandchildren and even friends. Even her grandchildren's friends would call her Nan and would always call upon her to make her famous cream puffs or sausage rolls at any party they were having.

In recent years, Beth's life had some difficult times, she lost her only great granddaughter and five years ago lost her daughter. The previous year she had lost her granddaughter. In addition to this, she had her own health issues which included bladder cancer two years prior, and more recently had battled kidney and bone cancer. Through all this she managed to keep providing love and support and had been a rock for those left behind. Despite all of her obstacles throughout her life, she was always there for other people. On the day of her passing I am told the entire family were by her side.

My lesson from Beth's story is this. It was very clear to me in this case that those who were loved the most, had the most love to give. It was such a privilege for me to have met this family and hear of her incredible strength and love.

I am blessed to meet and work with so many lovely

families where you build relationships very quickly. There are certain families that always stay with me, and this family is one of them. I was asked to conduct the service for Sid, who was ninety three years old when he passed. Fifteen months later, his wife Edna passed away. She was ninety one years old. It was an honour that the family asked for me to conduct Edna's *Celebration of Life* also.

Sid and Edna shared such an incredible love story. Sid lovingly called her *his blue-eyed girl*. Throughout their sixty-nine years of marriage they never spent a night apart up until she went into a nursing home. Sid absolutely adored her. She was the light of his life without a shadow of a doubt. They never went anywhere without the other and were always holding hands. Sid used to say it was to stop Edna from falling over, but everyone really knew the truth, they were inseparable.

They had a travelling lifestyle and lived in almost every corner of the globe. They began their married life in England living in several places. They came to Australia as ten-pound poms in 1961 with their three children. They lived in Adelaide for a little over three years, then moved to New Zealand, back to England, then to South Africa, back to

England, before returning and staying in Adelaide. They were a little like gypsies. As long as they were together that is all that mattered. Edna used to say that selling houses and moving kept them both young. They were wonderful role models to all of their family.

I am a big believer in fate and destiny. Sid's *Celebration of Life* was held in August 2017. Sid's memorial service at Eldercare (where he resided) was to have been held in that same month, however, for reasons outside of the family's control, the memorial service had to be postponed from August 2017 to 28th November 2018 – 15 months later.

It was fate that his wife Edna waited until November 2018 to leave this earth, and to have the 28th November 2018 as the day she was laid to rest. Her service was the *exact* same day as Sid's memorial service! Their daughter Christine told me they would have absolutely loved to have known they were being farewelled on the same day. Edna's favourite perfume was *Baronia*, so her granddaughter Sarah sprayed all of her clothes with it so she smelt lovely for when she and Sid were reunited later that day. At the end of Edna's service, I read a beautiful poem for Edna and Sid, who after fifteen months were now to be reunited. It

7 Life Lessons Learned Through Loss

read:

> *"The sadness they felt while they were apart*
> *Has turned into joy once more in each heart*
> *They embrace with a love that will last forever*
> *And side by side they are now again together."*
>
> Author unknown

What a beautiful love story. I have conducted several hundred *Celebrations of Life* for families grieving the loss of a loved one. In every service, I see LOVE in its purest form. I wish I could share all of them with you – you would be overwhelmed with the love that I see and hear. Death is LOVE.

As a result of this valuable life lesson, I founded a global movement called *The Love in Death* movement. This movement is changing the conversation around death, from fear to love, through focusing on love stories and the incredible life lessons that can be learned. I have been overwhelmed by the positive response all around the world and can see the difference this is making in so many people's lives.

As the Founder of this movement, I have created a

platform where individuals can share love stories and celebrate the life of their loved one; offering them the opportunity to heal and be reminded every single life has a meaning and a purpose.

You are invited to join *The Love in Death* movement. Become part of a community and movement that supports one another in their healing journey. There are two ways to join:

1) Visit my website www.sharonmuscet.com
2) Join *The Love in Death* Facebook Group

Gandhi said, "*In a gentle way, we can shake the world.*" I believe in a gentle way, we can do just that. In the learning of this valuable life lesson, Death is LOVE, and with the focus being on LOVE, we can aid in the healing of people all around the world.

I have recorded a video to inspire and support you. To learn more about this valuable life lesson, please visit my website -

www.sharonmuscet.com/resources/videos/7lifelessons/

Life Lesson 2:

Decide how you want to be remembered

Sharon Muscet

7 Life Lessons Learned Through Loss

We each make choices every day. Through the choices we make, we define who we are, we shape the life we want to live, and we shape how others see us. As Wayne Dyer suggests, *'As you think, so shall you become.'* How do you want to be remembered? What do you want people to say about you when you are gone?

I learned this incredible life lesson three years ago from a ninety six year old lady named Joan, who lived an extraordinary life. I never knew her yet, I wish that I had. I met with her family after she had passed, and heard all about her life. She had also written her own eulogy, something that doesn't happen very often. It was a privilege to have read her life story, in her own words.

This lady was the life of the party and a bundle of fun. She loved life and lived it to the absolute fullest. She had a great love of dancing which she still continued (and up on the table tops I might add) and really, the only reason she stopped was because the nursing home staff would no longer allow her to.

She was glamorous, vivacious and growing up loved the stage. She loved being the star on stage – singing, dancing and entertaining amongst so many other talents. She was awarded *The British Empire Medal* for bravery from King George. When she was very young, she was a hero in a fire, saving some children, and was in all the newspapers as well. She was described by her family as this shining light in everyone's lives. It was an extraordinary experience working with her family, and honouring the woman who had passed.

What was also extraordinary was her friend and neighbour Mishel, who was much younger and inspired by this woman and her life, put together an album of her life. I saw this album and it was like going on a trip down memory lane of the incredible life she lived and her achievements. I saw clippings from her time on Broadway, of the newspaper articles of her receiving her medal from King George, and other special times right though her life. It was incredible to be able to flick through and see all of this.

After the service, we followed the pall bearers outside to the hearse and watched as she was placed into it. She was then driven away to her final resting place. It was a peaceful experience. She had lived a good life. It had been a true celebration of her life.

7 Life Lessons Learned Through Loss

As people were saying their goodbyes, I had a number of them come up to speak with me. Many mentioned how I had captured the true essence of her nature in the service. It is certainly not difficult to do when I had such an incredible album of her history to go by. I had many people come up and tell me about her life. It was these words that changed everything for me. Words such as:

"I never saw Joan sad, ever."

"Joan always loved her champagne."

"Joan was always smiling."

"Joan was always the one up on the tabletops dancing, even in the retirement village!"

"She was always so friendly and would go up to any new people in the retirement village and say - Hello, I'm Joan, and introduce herself."

"She had this love of life."

I remember getting into my car after and I couldn't get the words of what the people had said to me out of my mind. What a wonderful way to be thought of. What incredible words to describe this lady. These words really got me thinking - *How do I want to be remembered? How* am I playing out in life? and What do I want people to say about me when I am gone?

This day happened at a time in my life when my marriage of twelve years had ended five months earlier. I was going through a very sad time in my life. Prior to this I had my very happy life – I had overcome my accident and was now married with my two children, two successful businesses, many friends, fun times and laughter. I loved being a Mum. I got so much enjoyment from my children. Life for me felt amazing.

However, sitting here in the car this day, I couldn't help but think, *If I was to die today, during this difficult time in my life, what would people say about me? How would I be remembered? Would it be things like:*

"Poor Sharon, she died so sad."

"Oh, it's terrible what happened to her in the past several months."

"Life wasn't fair to Sharon."

"Sharon had to overcome so many hurdles."

This was certainly what I felt I was projecting out to people at that point in my life, that was for sure. This day had been the biggest wake up call for me. For I would want people to talk about me like they had about Joan.

It made me recall one of my favourite quotes from Dr Wayne Dyer - *When you change the way you look at things, the things you look at change.* In an instant, just like that, I changed the way I saw life and in turn, that changed the way people saw me.

I left that service with a totally different attitude about me and my life. It is really up to me to create my life, and live it to the absolute fullest like Joan did. It got me thinking so many things. Life is so fragile and we can be taken at any time. This day had such an impact on my life. From that moment on I changed the way I saw life and I changed the way people saw me. I do not take a day for granted. I want people to remember me for all the good I have done in this world.

It was two years after learning this life lesson, when I visited my orthopaedic surgeon for one of my regular appointments since my accident. This day I shared with her how I was writing this book. She was interested to hear one of the life lessons, so I shared with her this story of Joan and the section on *Decide how you want to be remembered.* I shared with her how I thought I had been projecting myself to people.

My Doctor looked me straight in the eye and said, *"Sharon, you want to know how I would remember you?"* She said, *"I see a strong, independent woman; a woman who has chased her dreams and is changing the world; an amazing mother who sacrificed so much for her children; someone who overcame so much loss with poise and grace, and changed her life for the better. That's how I would remember you."*

I was speechless. Tears welled up in my eyes. A lump appeared in my throat. All I thought of was Joan and the lesson she instilled in me this day, two years ago. This day I decided how I wanted to be remembered, and in turn it changed the way people now remember me. Through Joan's love of life and through Joan's loss of life, she left me a legacy. I will be forever grateful to Joan for instilling this valuable life lesson in me.

Another wonderful story I wanted to share is with a man named Alan. He passed away suddenly at the age of seventy nine years. He was a devoted husband to his wife and wonderful father to his four children. He was exceptionally close to all of his grandchildren.

His was another story which reflects *Decide how you want to be remembered.* Of the people I met who spoke of him, he was the type of man who went out and made the most of all of the opportunities that were presented to him. His career in London, where he was born and raised, lead him to see a lot of the world when he was younger. The world was his oyster. When he was younger, he would sit at the London Docks where all the ships were and say, *"I'm going to be on one of them one day."* Sure enough, several years later, he joined the Merchant Navy and travelled around the world. From there he joined the Army for six years where he trained as a paratrooper. He used to watch movies with men jumping out of planes, so decided that is what he wanted to do. So, he went and did it.

He then became a Police Officer in London and became a Scotland Yard Detective. He worked in the Narcotics Division, then domestic violence, then homicide. You name it, he did it. At the age of thirty, with his wife and three young children in tow, they travelled from London to Australia because he decided he wanted a better life for his family. They were ten-pound poms. Times were tough when they first arrived, but together they made the most of their new life and soon called Australia home.

What struck me of this man was how nothing would stop him from going after what he wanted to do. When I spoke with his family, and then some friends after the service, I heard so many of the same things:

"Alan was a good father."

"Alan was a good provider."

"Alan was good at whatever he put his hand to."

"Alan was a no filters man."

"Alan liked a good chat."

"Alan wanted a better life for him and his family."

"Alan travelled the world."

"Alan had lots of experiences."

"Everyone loved him."

There were glowing praises for this man. I sat back again and thought, wow, what a wonderful way to be remembered. It was his love of his life first and foremost that I believe led to this. He went out and lived life. He said he wanted to be on the ships, and he did. He said he wanted to jump out of planes, and he did. He said he wanted a better life in Australia, and he went ahead, despite the obstacles. Once he arrived in Australia, he was unable to work for the Federal Police as his qualifications with Scotland Yard, even though he was very high up, were not recognised. In actual fact, the work he did whilst in Australia was not nearly as exciting as being in the Navy, jumping out of planes or being a Detective. But that wasn't what he was about. He decided he wanted a better life in Australia, and he set about doing that by providing for his family in any way he could. This man is a fine example of living your best life, despite any obstacles that comes your way. In living his best life, he was remembered in the highest regard.

So, I pose this question to you - *How do you want to be remembered*? Answering the below questions may help you with this, like they helped me.

- How do you want to be remembered?
- What do you want people to say about you?
- What impact do you wish to leave on your family, your work, the community, the world?

- What are your overriding strengths?
- How are you playing out in your life?
- How are you presenting to others right at this point in time? Are you happy with it?
- If your life ended right now, what did you love about your life?
- If you were given one more chance, what would you do differently?
- Have you achieved all that you want to achieve in your life?
- What is your legacy?
- What would be the five things you would want said at your funeral?

How are you behind closed doors?

Deciding how you want to be remembered also extends to this - Have you ever stopped and thought that how you present to the outside world, could be different to how you present behind closed doors?

You never know what goes on behind closed doors. You can think that a family or a person is so happy from the outside, yet behind those doors it is a very different story. How do you present behind closed doors? Do your loved ones see the very best version of you? Will they *remember* the very best version of you?

I met with a family and it was a different interview for many reasons. Most of the interviews I conduct with families can range from forty-five minutes to one and a half hours. Anything more can be too difficult for them at this time. I see myself as an *investigator* where I have a range of questions to ask. Whilst answering the questions, the family begins to share a whole range of wonderful memories and stories of their loved one whom has passed. It is always generally the same, I am greeted at the door. There is the loom of sadness spread amongst the house. I can feel the energy of the home as soon as I walk in. Often it is the home where the deceased has lived, or even passed away and you can feel that energy. There can often be a type of heaviness.

I am introduced to the family, and I make a mental note to remember all of the names I have been told. We sit, it is very quiet and often there are hands folded across their chest. I get it, why would you want a stranger walking into your house, to ask you about someone you were very close to. It is opening up deep wounds. It is about earning trust, and quickly. There is a real skill in doing so. It is about building relationships, connecting, finding a common ground or a common interest with the family. It is showing empathy and care. Tears are a natural thing and I encourage that as well. Again, I see that as having earned their trust where they feel comfortable to do this in front of me.

It generally does not take long for the trust between one another to be formed, and before I know it, the family are sharing so many stories with me, describing their loved one's nature and character. Often it is hard for me to keep up. It is the banter between the families that I am looking to capture and their loved one's life story. I know when they are sitting back, relaxing, smiling, remembering, that I have earned their trust and that they can open up to me.

I can always sense when it is time to depart, the pain of remembering starts to get too much for them and I swiftly leave. Promising them a draft of the service for them to look through in the days prior to the service. I want to ensure it is exactly how they want it.

On attending the family this day, I met with the daughter of their elderly mother who had passed. No other family members were able to attend. I had been briefed by the Funeral Director this family wanted a very simple service. I had also been told that they really hadn't wanted to open up about their mother to them. On this day, the interview was over within twenty minutes. I used my skills in asking many questions, however, there was not much information the family wished to share with me.

What I do find can happen, is that the final few months, or even years, when a family member is sick, can be very trying on families. Days going back and forth to the nursing home or hospital can be trying for them. Often, they see their family member in pain or losing their memory and it can sometimes feel a relief when they pass.

I didn't find any of that in this case. She simply did not wish to share any memories. She told me of a difficult upbringing and allowed me to read a short eulogy she and her siblings had prepared.

This service took me a considerable amount of time longer to write, yet it was quite a bit shorter. Why? It made me really sit back and reflect on their life, on this lady's life, and how you can live to your mid-nineties, yet, the people closest to you have not much to say about you. I reflected on what would have transpired for this to have happened? Is it that the pain for her children is just too much to bear? Or is it that there are no happy memories at all?

I recall doing another service, eight years ago. The family also had requested a simple service. When I sat with the four children, they started to share their life and their mother's life. Their father was an alcoholic and had passed away some years earlier. The children, even as adults now, were relieved about that. They were also relieved at their mother's passing, mainly as it was the end for them of a chapter they all wanted to forget. I could tell they were wanting to put the bad memories behind them. I heard that their mother had endured years of domestic abuse at the hands of their alcoholic father. I heard the stories of them as children hiding whilst this happened. I heard how their mother used to take the beating instead of it being taken on her children. I heard a story of how he chased her around the backyard with an axe, and threw it, missing her by inches. Some stories just never leave me, as I am sure they have never left those children.

They wanted no niceties at the funeral. It was to be just a formal process for them. For the pain of what their mother had endured was just too much for them to go through, and rather than bring those feelings to the surface, it was better to tuck them away deep and forget. I remember the day of this lady's funeral, there were many of her friends from the nursing home there. She had moved in after her husband's death, so they were not aware of her years of torment. She kept that hidden behind her closed doors. She had been a popular lady at the nursing home and made many friends. The service had only gone for ten minutes, and was the shortest I have ever done. The family wanted no readings, no eulogy, no reflection time, no committal, no petal tributes at the end. They really didn't want me to say much at all.

I could see the pain in their eyes the whole way through the service. I see it as my role to look out for these families during the service, to keep account of the pain they are going through. I have been known to cut out a reading or some paragraphs, if it appears the loved one is in too much intense pain. Their health and wellbeing are at the fore front of my mind. I remember seeing faces of the friends from the nursing home when I announced it was the end of the service. It had seemed like it had just begun, yet

I was already concluding it without any of the usual formalities. Their perception of this lady's life to her friends was far different to the family's. They did not know the pain which was inflicted behind those closed doors.

The lady I had recently met with was a lovely lady. Her siblings, who I met on the day of the service, equally as lovely. I met the grandchildren and great-grandchildren, nieces and nephews on the day of the service also. For a lady who lived to her mid-nineties, she had quite a few people attending the service. You often can find the older they are when they pass, the less people attend as most of their friends have already passed on.

As I met with them, I could see the grief on many people's faces. I heard some lovely stories of their grandmother. A granddaughter shared how sad she was, this was her first funeral and she wasn't sure how she would be able to cope. I met with our one and only speaker, besides myself, who was so warm and loving towards her Aunty who had passed. I had been told no family would wish to go in and view her, however, many did and there were many tears prior to the service.

I instinctively knew that there were many people there

with different experiences and perspective than the daughter I had met with just days prior. Their relationships with this lady were all so varied and different to the one that I had been told. I had been told there were no fond memories at all. No family holidays. No showering of love.

When it was time for me to invite this lady to talk, she was just wonderful. She really made the service with her incredible stories and memories of her Aunty. She spoke of how her Aunty's eyes used to sparkle when she greeted any visitors at the door.

That's when it really hit me. We all see people differently. Our own shared experiences with one person can be so varied. What one person's perception of a situation is, can be quite different to another. It also got me thinking that you truly never know what goes on behind closed doors. The stories I heard from this lady of her Aunty's eyes sparkling when she greeted visitors is vastly different to the stories I heard of a mother whom would embarrass her children every time they went out in public.

I am certainly not here to judge any family or any situation. I am merely here to be of service to them. To bring peace to this family in their time of need. I am here to celebrate a person's life, and through my written and spoken words, share what their life was about, what their meaning and purpose was. I am here to bring peace to all of those who came to farewell this lady.

Every single service I leave a richer person. I take all of them as a learning. I look at it as a life lesson. And so I did in this case. That day, I posed the question to myself – *How am I at home with my boys? How am I to the outside world? Is what happens behind closed doors a reflection on what I am showing to the world at large? Are my eyes sparkling for my boys like they are for those outside in the world, or even more?*

At this lady's funeral I looked at her photographs on her coffin. In one photograph she was young, in her early twenties. She looked so pretty and youthful. There was another photo of her taken most recently, in her ninetieth year. She looked hardened, with pursed-lips. I thought to myself what had happened throughout those years for people to have such different experiences with her? It got me thinking - *Do we ever truly know a person? Do we know their experiences? Are we too quick to judge?*

Often, we can treat those we love the most, the worst.

Often, we can smile to strangers we pass in the street, the person at the deli or the supermarket and make idle chat. When we arrive home, to our sanctuary, it is where we show our true selves. Whether that be good or bad, we need to ask the question – *What would our loved ones say about us when we depart? How are we appearing to them? Is that a reflection of our true selves? Are we coming from a place of love?*

So, my life lesson I learned is this:

How am I behaving behind closed doors? How will my loved ones remember me? Am I showering with love those who mean the most to me, or is it the work colleague, the person at the door, in the street or a total stranger who receives the most amount of my time, attention and love?

We all are responsible for our behaviour behind closed doors, and also to the outside world. Hold those loved ones close. Tell them daily of your love for them. Save the biggest sparkle in your eyes for those who you cherish the most, not for others at your door.

I have seen the effects of when it is not. I saw the children, heartbroken that day they laid their mother to rest. It wasn't that they had nothing nice to say. They had broken hearts. I saw the look on their faces asking, "Why? *Why was it that you were so kind to others, yet not kind to us?*"

Decide how you want to be remembered, *especially* to those behind your closed doors, and live your life by this.

Choose to make your life time one that is filled with great beauty, accomplishments, wisdom, caring and giving so that at end of your days, you may proclaim proudly and joyfully: *No regrets! I lived my life to my fullest*. Enjoy your magnificent journey and be more than you ever dreamed you could be… every day, every minute, every second. Life is so very precious.

I have recorded a video to inspire and support you. To learn more about this valuable life lesson, please visit my website -

www.sharonmuscet.com/resources/videos/7lifelessons/

Life Lesson 3:

What it truly means to live your best life

Sharon Muscet

7 Life Lessons Learned Through Loss

"I shall pass through this world but once.
Any good therefore which I can do or any
Kindness that I can show to any human being,
Let me do it now. Let me not defer or neglect it.
For I shall not pass this way again."

Stephen Grellet

Undoubtedly, one of the most powerful life lessons I have ever learned is this one - *What it truly means to live your best life.*

In this line of work, I meet so many families, and have the privilege of hearing incredible tributes. At a difficult time having lost a loved one, people stand before one another, and share from their heart. They share stories and memories. Some are funny. Some are incredibly sad. Some are long, some are short. They share poems. They sing songs. I have had people dance in the aisles to their favourite song. I have had choirs sing, football anthems played. Photographic presentations played. All equally meaningful, personal and from the heart.

I will never forget the service I conducted for Duane, who was forty five years old when he passed away. During his *Celebration of Life*, there were so many people who came forward to share tributes of Duane. This day moved me beyond belief for I heard the most powerful words in his tributes I have ever heard for a young man. Tributes like:

"Duane was a very sensitive, caring and intelligent man whom it was impossible not to create a strong connection with."

"Duane taught us fundamental lessons in life."

"The power within Duane gave us all strength, passion, love and unity."

"Duane lived life on his terms."

"We will never meet a man like Duane again in our lifetime."

"Duane was a complex contradiction of a man: incredibly strong, yet unassuming. A fierce fighter yet a passive, spiritual man."

There were many other words used to describe this extraordinary young man: unconditional love, acceptance, compassion, empathy, laughter, courageous, beautiful, humorous, peaceful, tranquil. That is some list!

Duane was a man of incredible standing. A man of incredible character, who had deep respect and adoration from all the people he came into contact with. Duane was studying religion at the time he passed away. He wanted to be of service and to change lives.

It was the impact Duane had on other people that blew me away the most. I have never heard such heartfelt tributes for anyone in the eight years of work that I have done. The love and adoration in that room at his *Celebration of Life* was remarkable.

There is something that you don't yet know about Duane. He had the most amazing gift I have ever heard of. He had the gift of communication.

But only through his *eyes*.

You see, Duane spent his whole life unable to speak, unable to eat, confined just to his bed and a wheelchair. Duane was fed his entire life through a PICC line. Duane had cerebral palsy.

When Duane was sixteen years old, the home that he lived in that looked after him, closed, and the family lost all trace of him. They tried unsuccessfully to locate him due to the new privacy laws. It took eleven years before they were reunited with Duane. He underwent a number of medical procedures and being the tough fellow that he was, he survived them all. He was a fighter, of that there is no doubt.

Up until this time of hearing Duane's story, I honestly thought living your best life was about a bungy jumping, sky diving, karaoke singing, travelling the world, scuba diving and that kind of thing. But it's not that at all.

The fundamental life lesson I have learned is this:

Living your best life is about the *impact* you make in this world.

It's about how you *choose* to live each day of your life despite your obstacles. Look at Duane. He spent his whole life in his bed.

And it's about *living every single day like it is your last*. Duane chose to fight and never give up, and live each day like it was his last. He had an urgency about making an impact in this world.

Duane made choices every day about how he lived. About how he treated other people and made them feel, despite his obstacles. He lived the best life that he could. Even though Duane's body did not respond in the way that most of our bodies respond, one thing that was evident was that you could not take away his mind.

Duane still got to make choices every day about how he lived his life. He chose to live it to the full. He made choices about how he treated other people. About how he made other people feel. About his willingness to fight and never give up, despite his obstacles. About how compassionate and empathetic he was towards other people. About the love he chose to give. About acceptance of his condition. Duane was a person of impeccable character. It was such a privilege for me to have heard his life story. Through Duane's loss of life, he left me a legacy. A legacy on what it *truly* means to live your best life.

Duane's story brings to mind a wonderful poem called *Desiderata* by Max Ehrmann which has impacted my life so much. Latin for *Desired Things,* there are so many great lessons we can all learn from this.

It is such a wonderful poem for everyone to see life in its brightest light. Each verse talks about hope, motivation and lessons learned through life. Each verse gives us a little advice on living in peace and harmony. The last verse is amazing – it summarizes everything about life:

"With all its sham, drudgery, and broken dreams,
it is still a beautiful world.
Be cheerful.
Strive to be happy."
Max Ehrmann, Desiderata, Copyright 1952.

Whatever problems you are experiencing today, always remember, that those failures will soon be a condiment that will give your success its flavour. It's still a wonderful life to live. You are blessed every day. Strive to be happy.

Live a life of gratitude

Do you believe in fate? I do. I am a believer that things happen for a reason. The following is a story about fate, which in turn led me to learn an important lesson about gratitude. Back in 1990, I worked part-time for Fosters and was a Fosters Girl at the Formula 1 Grand Prix in Adelaide. I did this over the four days that the world-wide race was held, over four consecutive years. It was back in the day when I was young and used to do some modelling work part-time for extra cash. They were fun times and I certainly got to experience another side of life!

I recall it was the 500th Grand Prix and Nelson Piquet actually won that race and I was surprisingly the grid girl that stood near him before the race. I happened to be down on pit straight afterwards for the celebration. He had the celebratory, victory champagne bottle and was squirting it around over everybody. I then recall seeing him hand it to someone over the fence, along pit straight. This man drank from the bottle. Never ever have I thought about that moment again. Until now.

I met with a family who had suddenly lost their husband and father. He was 89-years old. He had two sons. I connected with them and their mother immediately. As I asked them questions about their father and his life, they shared a story with me of one of the highlights of his life. It was in 1990 when Nelson Piquet won the 500th Formula 1 Grand Prix in Adelaide. They shared with me that their father was handed the champagne bottle by Nelson Piquet over the fence along pit straight and drank from it. My mouth dropped.

They saw my disbelief and questioned me on why my

mouth was wide open. I said to them, "*I was there. I actually saw that happen.*" The family couldn't believe it. I shared with them my story of why and how I happened to be there that day, and exactly what I saw. It seemed we had so many other things where we just connected. His wife had shown me when I visited their house a book of quotes and memes that she had kept for many years. Her boys did not actually know she kept this, until she got it out and showed it to me. I shared with her that I too have a book of quotes and do the very same thing as her.

Later that evening, I had emailed the family the draft of the service and his eulogy. The son returned my email with a response. He said, "*We cannot believe that story that you were at the same race and you actually saw one of the highlights of our Dad's life. We believe in fate and there was a reason that happened, and there is a reason that you have been sent to us to help us tomorrow.*" They stated they were just so happy and that their Dad would have loved me. To hear that meant the absolute world to me.

During the service, my heart broke for them. This was a very sudden death so the grief was evident. They are an extraordinary family. After the service, I stayed and had a cup of tea with them and the guests. Most of them had left and I was with the wife of the husband who had passed. She is an amazing lady.

Whilst we were talking after the service, she was holding my hand and she told me she didn't want to let me go. In fact, she told me she wanted to take me home with her! Her boys had said to her, *"Mum you need to let her go now!"*

It is not often that I am speechless nor my breath is taken away but what happened next did both. I was handed the most magnificent bouquet of white roses. The family, through their own grief and one of the most difficult times of their life, handed me this bouquet of roses. They had asked the Funeral Director to dismantle the wreath on top of their father's coffin and make up a bouquet for me. The two sons handed it to me and said, *"thank you for all you have done for us."* I wanted to burst into tears. I was so touched by their generosity and I certainly felt their love.

I thought about this family in turmoil and in utter shock and grief. Yet they could still find it in their heart to say *thank you*. They had so much gratitude for what I did, that they gave me these roses. They said, *"we wanted you to have these, and our Dad would have wanted you to have these for what you did for us today. We will never forget what you did for us."* They said they also felt that connection that I had with their Dad. I cried on the way home. That right there is an example of *The Love in Death*.

Since I had met this family the day before, I had thought of them. I couldn't get them out of my mind. She was a mother with her two sons. I am a single mother with my two sons. These men just adored their mother and adored their father. I thought, *What is it? What have they done that their family is so close, because I want that. That is exactly what I want for my boys and I, when they too grow into men.* I couldn't put my finger on it. There has obviously been a lot of love and they have been a close family, but there has to be more. Then it dawned on me the moment they gave me those roses. It is gratitude.

This family live a life of gratitude, and that really is it. In one of their darkest times, they still showed gratitude. They could still stand outside of their own grief, and truly be grateful for me. I was blown away by that. In times of hardship or stress, it can often seem difficult to be grateful. However, if we really think about it, we do all have something to be grateful for. Even it is a simple *thank you*, we are practising gratitude. My lesson in this – Live a life of gratitude.

It is about showing gratitude for life, for everything, for the simple things. Those roses meant everything to me. They were the most heartfelt gift I had received in a very long time. Those roses ended up being a bigger gift than intended – for they were a living example of gratitude.

The power of gratitude can actually rewire your brain to be compassionate, which in turn makes you feel good. That simple act of gratitude by this family, at one of the most difficult times in their life, even for a brief moment, would have brought some joy into their life. The more you look around in your life, the more you can be grateful for. This positivity extends to others around you, creating an incredible virtuous cycle.

Fate certainly played a part in me learning this lesson. Who would have thought, back in 1990, I was there to witness one of the greatest moments in this man's life and then I was there to lay him to rest. Gratitude is an essential part of life. Give and you shall receive.

Sharon Muscet

I have a gratitude journal at home, I write in it each day. My boys have a gratitude journal as well and I teach them about gratitude. This has significantly increased my sense of happiness and well-being. Being grateful for the simple things in life. By instilling this in my children, I hope they grow into the fine men that I had the privilege of meeting. I hope I will be a mother like the beautiful woman I had the pleasure to meet. There really is a beautiful side to death.

Another story I heard about gratitude, which has never left me, is of a sixty three year old woman. She was married and had two boys. It was only upon her passing that one of her sons discovered a journal that his mother kept and wrote in regularly. It was a *Gratitude and Blessings* journal that she would write in every other day. She would write about all the things she was grateful for, life's simple pleasures, such as her healthy children, her warm bed, her home and her garden. They allowed me to read a few of her pages and what struck me was how at peace she seemed in her world, and how happy she was with life. Her love of life just oozed through the pages.

One such verse the family enjoyed reading – and asked

me to share on the day of her service – was written by her on Anzac Day in 2011 – it was six years before she passed away. It is an entry which holds great significance to the family and gives you an insight into her thankfulness to those brave men and women. She wrote:

"Observing the day and date – one thousand blessings for the men who fought for my freedom. Unfathomable gratitude for their courage, honour and belief in their country and its citizens, and their right to freedom."

There really is no better practice than gratitude, which is something this lady lived her life by. She continued to practice gratitude, even in the toughest times of her cancer treatment. It is what kept her strong and positive. I am told she also kept many inspirational quotes and poems which the family also found amongst her belongings. One such quote was placed on the back of her memorial card handed out at the service:

Sharon Muscet

"Attract what you expect
Reflect what you desire.
Become what you respect
And Mirror what you admire."

(author unknown)

Living a life of gratitude is one of the greatest things you can ever do for your own peace of mind and your own happiness. Learning of these lessons from these two families shows me that even in their darkest hours, by showing gratitude, they didn't suffer. Rather they left their truest gifts upon this world.

Be there for others

I learned three amazing lessons from a funeral service I conducted for an eighty three year old lady. I had done the service in the morning and by the end of the day, I felt like a changed person.

This lady had never married and did not have any children. However, she had a very loving family. She was loved dearly by her nieces and nephews and her great niece. They spoke so highly of her. Her eulogy was powerful. They talked about her overriding strength which was to care and support other people and to be there for others. It straight away had me thinking – *what is my overriding strength? What would be the one thing people would say is mine?*

I ask you to consider this question too - *What is your overriding strength?* What is the one thing that people would say is yours? Think about that and think about the way in which you live your life. It started me thinking and became a valuable lesson. I went home and asked my two boys, *"What is the thing you think about most, when you think about Mummy?"* I asked them this at separate times and they had both answered along the same lines of, *"You are so kind and caring and give the best hugs."*

I considered it further and yes, I see my overriding strength as being my empathy as well as my kindness and compassion for others (as well as my hugs!). What is yours? Ask your loved ones around you. It is an interesting exercise. My boys then asked me the same question of what I saw their overriding strength as being, and so I was able to share what I saw most in them.

It was straight after this service, a lady came up to me and said, *"Sharon, I am deaf and I have a cochlear implant.*

Sharon Muscet

This was the first funeral that I have ever attended that I have been able to hear the whole service in its entirety. Thank you so much. You were amazing." Those words made my day. It touched my heart. I said to her, *"You don't know how much that means to me to hear that."*

We don't know what is going on in other people's lives. She did not know that I had a couple of things happen to me that morning that I had been feeling quite sad about. I was there to present the service so appeared confident and strong. It had made my day that she had said this to me. It's like she knew I needed to hear some kind words. I thought how wonderful of this lady, she didn't have to do it, to just come up and say this beautiful gesture.

After the service I got myself a cup of tea and was speaking with some of the guests in the lounge. I saw the same lady standing in the corner on her own, so I went up and started chatting to her. We talked about her, about her deafness, and we then talked about other parts of her life. I was present and I really listened to her.

She then shared with me that three months prior she had lost her husband to cancer. She also shared that one month prior to his passing, her son had also died to the same cancer. She was very teary and what struck me, was this lady needed someone to listen. So, I stood and held the space for her. I was so moved by her words.

What I was blown away most by was, here is a lady who only three months ago lost her husband and four months ago lost her son. She is going through a very difficult time. Yet she still managed to come up and pay me a compliment. She still showed gratitude to the little things in her life. It is not hard to connect with people, it's about paying it forward in any way you can. She offered me a simple compliment. We then built a relationship. It was about listening and holding the space for her.

Isn't it amazing to know that you can just connect with people and that is the thing in any of the work that I do, it is just building relationships. It is connecting with people, it is listening to people and it's paying it forward in any way you can.

So, these were my lessons I learned from this one service:

Always pay someone a beautiful gesture – you don't know what it will do to their day.

Just hold the space for someone and really listen. You don't know what people are going through in their life and they just need a kind and caring person. It is about truly being there for other people, caring and listening.

What is your overriding strength?

The simplest things matter in the end

I never liked being on my own. It is something that I am often faced with when my boys go to stay with their father, and yet it was something for a long time I just couldn't get used to. It wasn't until recently that I learnt to accept it.

In actual fact, it was in the writing of this book that I fully accepted it. I took myself away to my family's holiday home, on my own, for days, to complete my work. It was the first time since my accident fifteen years prior that I had been on my own. Was I frightened? You bet! Why? Many reasons.

Fear of the unknown in the writing of this book for starters. I also wondered how I would go on my own after being around my children for so long. And you know what? I totally loved it. I loved the complete freedom. I loved that I was doing something for me and also for others in the writing of this book. It has been one of the most healing things for me I have ever done. I had recently read a quote (author unknown) that said:

> *"You come home, make some tea,*
> *sit down in your armchair, and all around there's silence.*
> *Everyone decides for themselves*
> *whether that's loneliness or freedom."*

All this time I had seen myself as being lonely, yet really if I changed the way I looked at that, what I have is total freedom. The way I believe life should be lived.

One of my first memories I have of growing up is of total freedom. I grew up in the country with paddocks all around me. I felt totally free. As a little girl, I would run in the paddocks, amongst the sour-sobs, playing hide and seek chasey. I loved that feeling of laying on my back, looking up into the sky with the sun on my face. Here I was, freedom around me. Such a simple thing. It's just I had chosen to see it differently. I was looking at it as loneliness.

This lesson was again reinforced when I met with a

beautiful lady named Karen. She had just lost her father Doug. Theirs was a story of sacrifice, love and freedom. I learnt the most valuable lesson that it's not the material things that count, rather, it is the simplest of things that matter in the end.

Doug was a single parent and Karen was the love of her father's life. Doug was known to say many times to people, he had everything in his life he ever wished for in Karen. When Karen married her husband Shane, that then included Shane, and their daughter Maddison.

When Karen was little, she lived with Doug's parents in the country whilst Doug did all he could to provide for his daughter in the city – this was the ultimate sacrifice for Doug and one can only assume how much that must have broken his heart. Doug didn't drive so he would make his way by bus to see Karen on weekends and Karen recalls many happy memories of her and her father walking everywhere such as down the street and to the beach.

Doug was a very simple, no fuss type of man who did not want a spectacle of anything made. He was a man of few words and what he said, he said. He loved reading books, photography, going to the movies and lunching. He was a loner and did what he wanted to do when he wanted to do it. He lived by his roster and was a big planner – he liked to know where he was going and when. He was a creature of habit.

He enjoyed his companionship with a lady for a number of years and became very close to her family. Karen has some wonderful memories with all of them. He had few friends, and the ones he did have he was faithful and loyal to them all. He was a man of great integrity – his word was his word. If he said he would ring, he would ring at that time precisely on the dot.

One of his most favourite times was Grandparents' Day and visiting Maddison at school. At the start of the year he would be asking Karen when it would be, to ensure he kept the date free. He liked to come in the afternoon and be able to stay and be there when Maddison finished school. It was the highlight of his year. She tells me she called him *Little Pa* because he was quiet and little and any cards he gave to her, he always signed as *Little Pa*. They had a very special bond.

Another truly beautiful bond was with his good friend Geoff. He came into Doug's life as a St John's carer when the two were matched together over ten years ago. Karen, Geoff and Doug enjoyed many lunches together. It was always the same place, same table as Doug was that creature of habit. Who would have thought their friendship was to last as long as it did. Geoff mentioned to Karen that he believes it was he who looked forward to their catch-ups more than Doug in the end.

Doug wasn't one for crowds or group gatherings, preferring 1:1. He was quiet and reserved. Doug was never in a frazzle, he just went about his own way. Karen described him as a *gentle little muppet*. He never complained, never said boo when he was in hospital having his procedure for his melanoma. All he could think about was going out for lunch afterwards, his favourite thing to do.

Karen said people would think that Doug was a lonely man, but he was the exact opposite. He would say he was the luckiest person in the world – he had Karen, he had Shane and he had Maddison. He would always say how happy and fortunate he was in his life. He didn't worry about anything material – he believed he had it all.

He would say, "*I couldn't ask for anything else, what*

would I need?" Karen's wedding day was one of the happiest days of his life. When Maddison was born he said, *"What more could someone want, than to see a beautiful granddaughter."* He said he wanted to be around long enough to see her old enough and happy.

Doug had moved into a Nursing Home. In the last few weeks before he passed, he grew more frail and tired. He asked to see the Pastoral Care lady, which he had never done before, and asked her, *"Why am I here?"* She replied, *"Everybody has a different belief as to why they may be still here."* His reply was, *"I think I'm all good."* With that he passed away, peacefully. He lived a wonderful life. He was a loving, simple, honest and caring man who loved and was loved.

Doug lived by his own rules throughout this life. Even he decided when his time was right for him to leave this world. One could say on seeing him that he was a lonely old man. Yet he was known to have said he was the happiest man alive. He had everything he could ever wish for – his daughter, son-in-law, his granddaughter and his health.

He could go for two weeks and not see anyone, his carer Geoff told me. Yet he was never lonely. He loved his books, his reading, his Andre Rieu music, his photography, his lunches. The simple pleasures in life. He loved Grandparents' Day - that was the highlight of his year. He couldn't wish for more.

What I love about this story is that Doug had total freedom in his life. He made good of a bad situation when he became a single parent. He did all he could to provide for his daughter. He sacrificed his life for that of his daughter. He gave her everything he could. He chose to live his life alone, and yet he never felt alone. He had everything he could wish for.

The life lesson I learned from this:

It is the simple things in life in the end that matters. Doug was loved and he loved. The things he loved in life was all he needed. We often get caught up in the material things of life. Wanting more. Hunting down success. Wanting more money. Wanting that car, house, boat, overseas travel. But in the end, what is it that we really want? To love and be loved - and freedom.

This exert from a poem by Andrea Balt describes it beautifully:

"Freedom is about being so
Truly, madly and deeply
Attached to your own soul
That you can't bear –
If only for a moment –
A life that doesn't
Honour it."

Find your Tribe and love them hard

The second funeral service I ever conducted was for a man in his fifties. There were eleven people who attended his funeral. There was no family, only work colleagues. He had cancer, and yet no one at his work knew that. He had kept it to himself. He had passed away on his own in his unit, and it was four weeks later before he was to be discovered. His work had become worried as he hadn't returned from holidays, and so they phoned his neighbours who then went and checked.

I found that very sad and very confronting for my second funeral. To know there was a life that was lost, yet no one was there nor knew of his passing for some time. I remember wondering how it would have been for this man, to have left this world on his own. Was it his own choosing? Or did he feel he had nobody?

I recently heard of another very sad situation that a Funeral Director had told me about. A lady in her nineties had died in November 2017, however, her body was not discovered until six months later, in May 2018. She had two family members still living - her nieces. She wasn't close with them by any means, however, they were her next of kin. I found this so incredibly sad that for six months no one knew she was missing. No one had phoned her. No neighbours had checked on her. It was like she never existed. This was a life. A life that for over ninety years walked this earth and yet no one noticed she was gone. How can that be? It makes me so incredibly sad.

It also got me thinking about the need to find your Tribe. I don't know the situation around this man's life or this woman's life and why there was no one around them to care for them. Maybe it was their choice. It is not my place to make judgment. However, one of my biggest lessons from this was to *Find your Tribe and love them hard*. This is a motto I have always lived my life by. So, who is in your Tribe?

7 Life Lessons Learned Through Loss

I consider myself to be a very lucky person who has an incredible Tribe of people around me. There is a saying that goes, *Your Vibe Attracts your Tribe.* It is about surrounding yourself with like-minded people. I have a professional speaking mentor named Sam Cawthorn. He is an incredibly inspiring man who has taught me so much. One thing he has always said to me is *Proximity is Power.* You surround yourself with like-minded people around you, and you can't go wrong.

What I look for in my Tribe is those people who have your back, no matter what. That is first and foremost for me. People who are completely loyal, trustworthy, loving, kind, caring and considerate. It is all the qualities I see in myself that I look for in other people. It cannot be a one-way street. In order to have that Tribe around you, you too must share those same qualities and be that to those people as well.

Within my Tribe, I have what I call mini-Tribes. My mini-Tribes are made up of my Spiritual friends who share similar beliefs to me. Then I have my mini-Tribe of Friends who are just extraordinary. My Family mini-Tribe who are so dear to me. I have my Professional Speaking mini-Tribe who are all incredible people making such a difference in this world through their speaking journey. We all have a mission, a purpose and a passion to spread our message with the world. Then there are some other mini-Tribes, like my Business mini-Tribe, and the funeral celebrancy work that I do. There is a mini-Tribe made up of Funeral Directors whom I have the pleasure to work with every day. They are the most extraordinary people who are there to make a difference in people's lives. I have written all of my mini-Tribes down and put big love hearts around them.

Over the last couple of years, especially during the difficult time in my personal life, my Tribe has changed. People have come and gone from my Tribe, and that's ok. People come into your life for a reason, a season and a lifetime. Life is a cycle. It is about finding that core group of people and the Tribe that absolutely have your back. I am so grateful for my Tribe who I keep really close.

Ask yourself who is in your Tribe? Break it down to your mini-Tribe. Love them hard. Let them know that they are in your Tribe and how special they are to you. Treat them like gold. It is so important to have those loved ones around you, particularly in your time of need. You just don't know when you are going to draw upon those who you need. Time and time again, I am amazed by people who have their Tribe around them, at the time when it is needed the most, when they are departing this world.

One such lady I recall passed away suddenly when she was sixty years old. She was not married and did not have any children. I will never forget her mother during the service. I literally saw a broken heart this day. From the moment I said my first word to commence the service she sobbed. How I just wanted to be there for her.

Her brother summed it up to me when he said, "*look up the word LOVE and that was her, through and through.*" This lady had a huge Tribe around her. It got me thinking – was it the love that she gave and showed to others, that allowed her to have such a large Tribe around her? I was literally taken aback from the number of people who came to pay tribute to her. She was described as a loyal friend. I was told that her great strength above all else, was she loved her family. It was everything to her and she was inspirational in her devotion to her family. She was a loving daughter, sister, sister-in-law, Aunty, Great Aunty and Godmother to several children. She was actively involved in every single one of their lives. She loved life, she had so many passions, she gave anything a go.

I could not get over all of the loving tributes that people shared or wrote throughout the service. It got me thinking about her Tribe. She certainly loved her Tribe hard. Yes, she surrounded herself with them. However, do you know what made her Tribe so special?

- It was the love that she showed to others.
- It was the love that she had to give.
- It was always being there for other people.
- It was being the most amazing daughter, sister, friend, family member.

She put others before herself. She would always find time to attend birthdays, christenings, weddings, Christmas or just dinner. It didn't matter what State it was in, she would find a way to be there. She was selfless. She showed loyalty, kindness and compassion. She fully lived life. She had many passions. She had many interests. Some of them involved other people hence she made wonderful friendships. She would phone her elderly parents every single night and her father would always end the call with

7 Life Lessons Learned Through Loss

"*Night Babe*". She left behind a legacy of love for everyone and the family made a promise to keep that going for her.

There is a beautiful quote by Eden Ahbez which is:

*"The greatest thing you will ever learn
is just to love and be loved in return."*

This to me, is what makes up your Tribe. This is the life lesson I have learned. It is showing love and receiving love in return. The more you give love, the more love you will receive. So, when it matters the most, your Tribe are there, loving on you, being there for you, so that you will never have to be alone.

If there is one thing I have learnt in the last eight years, you need to live each day like it is your last. You don't know when your time to depart this earth is up. I have seen several hundred people lose their lives. Whether it is pre-birth, post birth as babies, childhood deaths, teenage deaths, young adults, middle age, the elderly. When your time is up, it is up. Even from my own near-death experiences, I have realised how fragile life is, and we really do need to live each day like it is our last.

There are a lot of families I have met with who have said their family member, "lived a good life." There are others who told me they were taken far too soon. They didn't get to live their life. They still had so much they wanted to achieve in their life time. What if you were told you had one day to live? Have you achieved all you wanted to do? Have you told all of those people important to you, what they mean to you? Would you have any regrets? I believe we do need to live each day as if it was our last day here on this earth.

Imagine a world where we would tell all of those people whom were important to us that we loved them each day. Imagine the world if we were all living out each day doing the things we loved most. Imagine the world if we all didn't sweat the small stuff or get caught up in pettiness, and just concentrated on what was truly important to us. What a different world it would truly be.

What if you were told you had one year to live. Would you do things differently to what you had planned? Would you quit your job and tick off a bucket list? I am a big believer in having a bucket list. I have one and I created two for my boys. It is a list of things that I want to achieve throughout my lifetime.

I have been filling this in regularly, and more importantly, ticking it off regularly. It is my goal in life to go out and do all of the things that are going to make my heart sing as well as create impact in this world. There are so many things that I want to achieve in my life.

One of my goals in life that is on my bucket list as item number five, is to be a published author. Whilst it is about ticking this off, most importantly it is a way of me to be of service to others. For several years I have wanted to write this book. The idea has always been there, I had just never got around to doing it. I used to always think - one day. One day never seemed to come around.

With the work that I do, seeing people losing their life, it constantly reminds me of living in the present and not wasting my time. Do the things that will make your heart sing. So, I went ahead and immersed myself into the publishing world, something until then was unbeknown to me, and started to live out one of my dreams. It has been one of the most fulfilling things to do in my life.

Sharon Muscet

My two boys write in their bucket list and also tick their bucket list off. What a wonderful thing to have instilled in them from a young age. Not only to dream, but to dream big, and then how to work towards their goals. To see them tick off some of these bucket list items is amazing.

I met with a family in early January 2016. They had lost their wife and mother at the age of fifty two years. Her family were everything to her. She had such a big heart. She was selfless, generous and a wonderful friend. She was also a wonderful listener whom was caring and compassionate and had a way of drawing people into opening up and talking to her. She created an impact in the lives of those around her.

She was very brave and had an incredible inner strength, overcoming some of her greatest fears. She lived her life right up until the very end. When she knew she was sick, she set out to tick off as many bucket list items as she could before she passed.

She was able to achieve many things from her bucket list. She was afraid of heights yet flew over the Grand Canyon. She wanted to go to Waimea Falls in Hawaii and actually swim out under the waterfalls. Even though she was quite weak, she was so determined to go and do this. She did get to Hawaii and did get to float and swim under the waterfalls that she wanted to. She said to her husband whilst doing this, "Ships are meant for sailing, not around safe harbours." How true that was. She really did live life up until the end.

I pose you this question - Would you live your life differently if you found out you only had a day or a year to live? If you answered yes to this question, then you are not living your best life.

What changes do you need to make to live your best life? Would you tell those people you loved the most how much they mean to you? If you were arguing with a person who meant the world to you, would it no longer have meaning?

Would you go out and pursue your passions? Would you do all those things that truly make your heart sing? Did you know when you are inspired to do something or inspired by something, you are – in-spirit – that is what inspired means. You are in your true essence. Go out and tick off the things that truly inspire you, tick off that bucket list. You just don't know which day will be your last day.

Go with no regrets; know that you have lived the very best life that you possibly could. Some people don't get to live long lives. You do. You are here for a reason and a purpose. Do you know what you are here for? Do you know what you are called here to do?

I do. I found it in my work as a Funeral Celebrant. I found it in the writing of this book. I found it in being a mother. I found it in truly being of service to other people. I found it in being an international speaker and sharing powerful messages, life lessons and love stories of those passed with a view to helping other people live their best life. How do I know I have found my calling? Because I feel inspired. I am in-spirit.

In summary, the valuable life lesson I have learned, from all of these stories, about what it means to truly live your best life is this:

Living your best life is about the IMPACT you make in this world.

It is how you CHOOSE to live every day of your life, despite your obstacles.

7 Life Lessons Learned Through Loss

It is about living a life of gratitude, truly being there for other people and living a life of freedom, not loneliness.

It is not the material things that count, rather, it is the simplest of things that matter in the end.

It is about finding your Tribe and loving them hard, ticking off those bucket list items and living your life in-spirit.

Finally, truly living your best life is about living every single day like it is your last. Gandhi said, "Live as if you were to die tomorrow." We all are here with a purpose. You only have now. There is no past, you create your future by living your best life now. The future is you. It is all in your hands. So, live your best life, NOW.

I have recorded a video to inspire and support you. To learn more about this valuable life lesson, please visit my website -

www.sharonmuscet.com/resources/videos/7lifelessons/

Life Lesson 4:

Dysfunction in families is normal

Sharon Muscet

Another important life lesson that I have learned is to do with dysfunction in families. This topic is something very personal to me and something I carried a lot of shame around for a long time. You see, I had a breakdown in my relationship, for a time, with my parents. We had not seen eye to eye on an issue and as a result, we were not speaking. We were always a happy family and close, so this breakdown was difficult for all of us.

The work I do as a Funeral Celebrant actually helped me to understand there are so many families going through similar situations with families not speaking. It led me to realise that dysfunction in families is *normal*. This realisation allowed me to release the shame I had been holding onto for many years, as well as begin to openly discuss it with close friends around me. This was a big part of my healing process.

There are many different types of dysfunction. I meet with families at the most vulnerable times in their life. I have seen arguments, doors slammed, harsh words spoken, and many tears. I see family members estranged from one another, and in some case for over twenty or thirty years.

In extreme cases we have had to have family members in separate rooms prior to the funeral commencing. On occasion we have had security and police on standby throughout the service. I have seen siblings verbally abuse one another around their mother's and father's graveside where we have had to step in and ask them to stop.

I have also seen families, who have not spoken for many years, come together on the day of the funeral and for a time, put aside their differences and be at peace with one another as they lay their family member to rest. I have seen families who even though they do not see eye-to-eye, be okay with one another getting up and speaking at the service, acknowledging each other.

My biggest learning is that dysfunction within families is a part of life. It is nothing to be ashamed of. It is what we do with the dysfunction, and how we handle it, that is more the issue. Very often I meet with families and they share about the estrangement or dysfunction in their family. It is much the same, they carry a sense of shame and embarrassment when they share this with me. When I share with them that through my experience, I have found that dysfunction is *normal*, or when I am talking with friends who have dysfunction within their family, and share this life lesson, I see their shoulders drop, and their own shame lifted. I believe it is important for us all to get past this shame.

From the dysfunction I have seen within the families I have met and my own family dysfunction – I can tell you that dysfunction is all borne out of LOVE. I can sit with a family and I see their hurt, I see their anger, I see their pain and I see their frustration. The list goes on. At one point they loved each other. That's why dysfunction can hurt so much. There is still love there for one another somewhere. It may not be the love that once was there, it has changed now, but love underlies it all.

What I wish you to consider in this life lesson, is that once our loved ones have passed on, we cannot turn back the clock. If you are in a dysfunctional relationship with a family member or someone close to you, the question I ask is, "Will *you have regrets after they are gone?*" There is no right or wrong here. What I pose through my learnings is that you look at the various angles of dysfunction.

Sharon Muscet

My Story with Dysfunction and having no regrets

Whilst I don't wish to go into the situation with myself and my parents, know this: it broke my heart. And, it was all borne out of LOVE. I suffered shingles at the time of the breakdown of my relationship with my family. I will never forget the stress it caused. I cannot turn back the clock. It is what it is and is part of my life's journey and a part of my life story.

I can say that without doing this funeral celebrancy work, and the lessons I have learnt around dysfunction, I may never have reached out to members of my family, in an attempt to rebuild our relationship. I guess sometimes hurt, anger and frustration block the overall picture.

Sometimes it is hard to make your way through the anger of what you are feeling. Sometimes, it is time that is the only healer. However, when we look at life and death, we don't have time. There is no time to waste. Life is so fragile. There are no guarantees.

I remember the countless times I would meet with a family. Perhaps it was their mother whom had died, and the siblings were all together recalling fond memories of her. I would be delivering a service and the son would come up and deliver an incredible eulogy for his father. I would watch the DVD presentation - the *Celebration of Life* with many photographs of the happy family. I couldn't help but have a sense of sadness come over me and grieve the loss of my own relationship with my family.

This had happened many times for me, but what struck me was a service for a man named Lionel. He was eighty six years old when he passed. The family shared many stories that reminded me so much of my own father. He was a country man. A man of great standing within his community. He was a larger than life character who was big in stature. He was a man's man and at the same time, a gentle-man. He loved a beer with the boys, was a true gentleman, and always displayed respect and courtesy towards women. He had a quick wit and was known for his one-liners. He was a driven man who was hardworking and had magnetism where people were drawn to him. He was a very welcoming man who would put his arms out to you and you couldn't help but be drawn in. He was a man who was quick to the point, if there was a short way to do it, he would do it! Everything about him reminded me of my own father.

His son, John, was introduced to read the eulogy. We were in a very large chapel and there would have been about two hundred people in the room. I sat behind John and listened intently as he delivered the Eulogy. I am always so drawn to people's life stories. As the words rolled out of John's mouth, I couldn't help but be drawn to his words. The love, adoration and respect he had for his father was so evident. As he talked about his father, I couldn't help but think, *"What if my father passed away right now? How could I deliver his eulogy when we are no longer speaking?"* There was such a pain that rushed over me at that moment. I had to suddenly switch those thoughts off and come back to the space I was in so I could continue to lead the service.

I could not stop thinking about it for days afterwards. What if that was my Dad? Would I have regrets at not speaking to him? The answer to that question came to me immediately. Of course I would have regrets. I would regret all the time I missed with my father. I would regret not being able to stand before a congregation and talk about the man who gave me life, and who I loved.

John's words that day really changed me and I will be

forever grateful. He did not know that the delivery of the eulogy of his father that day was the catalyst for me then reaching out to my mother and father just days after. Was I scared to do so? Yes. Did I fear rejection? Yes. Am I glad I did? Absolutely, yes.

Little did I know that day my mother had been sitting in her lounge room chair, at lunchtime, thinking of me. She later was to tell me she had said a prayer asking, *"how do I get back in touch with Sharon?"* For it seems all this time her heart was breaking too. She didn't know how to reach out to me. She wasn't sure I would be wanting to talk to her.

Isn't it incredible that two grown women, both had their hearts breaking, yet both didn't know how to reach out to the other. Both were thinking the other didn't want to speak. Both were so wrong. One can only wonder how many other families this is happening to?

This is the thing about dysfunction, often in the end we do not know what we are arguing about. Often it is just pride that comes and gets in the way. Too proud to say I'm sorry. Too proud to say let's wipe the slate clean. Too proud to say let's try again. The moment I reached out to my mother and my father we were reconnected. There were many tears and within a week they had come to the city to visit my children and I.

It was six months after reconnecting with my parents that my father was diagnosed with cancer. I cannot tell you how grateful I was that I could be there for him in his time of need. It was a healing time for our relationship. I spent many hours with him and my mother in hospital – the most time I had spent with them in a very long time. It is amazing what can happen in times of need and when we realise we are dealing with life and death.

Over the next six months, as my father underwent intensive chemotherapy treatment, we were able to set healthy boundaries and fully appreciate where each other was at. I am so grateful for the life lesson I learned the day that I heard the powerful delivery of Lionel's eulogy, that prompted me to call my parents. It has changed the course of not only my life, but my children's as well.

Time and time again in the line of work that I do, I realise that life is so fragile. We truly do need to live each day like it is our last. Life can change or be taken from us at any time and our relationships with loved ones should never be taken for granted.

As I had mentioned, the shame that I have carried for many years was great. The funeral celebrancy work has allowed me to see that dysfunction in families is in fact, normal. It is normal for families not to see eye-to-eye. It is normal for families to have rifts. It is normal for family members to be different. So many times, I have met families and they would say to me how ashamed they are that there are family members not talking. So many times I would sit in a meeting with families during conflict. The death of a family member is emotional at the best of times, but add some dysfunction as well and it can often be heightened. Perhaps that is why I do this work and am called upon to work with these families, because I totally get it and would tell them that.

I would say to them, *"there is no need to apologise. The work I have done over the years has shown me that dysfunction is normal."* I would also explain to them that there was, in fact, dysfunction and conflict within my own family. I would see the weight on their shoulders lifted. What I see is that family members do love and care for one another. Often, we don't have the tools to know how to deal with our deep emotions for one another, particularly when there is conflict. There is so much emotion involved.

I am so grateful that I have been able to see firsthand these lessons in family conflict and dysfunction. The weight of the world was lifted off my shoulders, particularly when dealing with shame. It allowed me then to start talking to those closest to me about it to aid in my own healing. This in turn then helped me in having the courage to come forward and reach out to my parents.

I undertook a funeral service for a lady who was ninety three years old. She had lived a difficult life, having found her mother at the tender age of eleven, collapsed and dead at the bottom of the stairs. This event and giving birth to a stillborn baby was to torment her in later life. She got through the second world war in her teenage years always scared of going home in the dark because of the blackouts. She experienced the coronation of the Queen and met her husband at the end of the war in the dance hall.

She had married the love of her life and they were married for fifty-four years before his passing. She loved her family and life for her was all about them. In her later years, she was remembered for her strength in fighting injury and illness. She got through fractured hips, falls, pneumonia, chest infections and always rallied around. She always had the resilience to pull through. One of her daughters shared with me she is one of the strongest people she has ever known.

At the time when this lady passed away, her two daughters were not speaking and had not been for some time. She had accepted that. She had made it clear to her two daughters that she loved them equally. It was important to her that her girls knew that, especially at the end of her life.

On the day of the service, and having gone through my own conflict within my own family, I couldn't help but feel for the two daughters who were sitting on either side of the chapel. They clearly loved their Mum, of that there is no doubt. Both were absolutely delightful in dealing with and in how they spoke of their mother. Both were very respectful of one another and of one another's wishes for how the funeral service was to go. My heart goes out to them for I do know that conflict in families is hard, particularly at a time now when they are grieving the loss of their mother. What I said to them both, as they apologised to me for this conflict was, "*dysfunction is normal, it is okay, you don't need to apologise.*" It was important that they release the shame.

We should never judge. It is about holding the space, listening if needed, and being of service to them and to their mother.

I was once asked to lead a service for a father and husband who had passed away. His daughter described him as the strongest and bravest person she had ever known. For over twenty years he had lived with Crohn's disease and cancer for two years, yet, through it all he touched the lives of so many people.

He was born in Greece and as a teenager his family decided to take the plunge and make a life for themselves in Australia. He was in his twenties when he met the love of his life, an Australian girl, whom he charmed with his wit and his humour. Six months after meeting they were engaged and three years later, he married his soul mate. It was not long after this they moved from Sydney to Adelaide and they had their daughter. She was his little girl and the apple of his eye. They were inseparable. They were always together having an adventure.

7 Life Lessons Learned Through Loss

He was the eldest of three boys and his two brothers were his closest friends. He cherished his father, mother and brothers. He adored his mother-in-law, brother-in-law's and sister-in-law's, uncles, aunties and cousins, nephews and nieces. Through all his love for his family, it was his wife and daughter who were his world.

His final wish was that he have a civil service. His wife and daughter were there to carry out his wishes. However, being Greek, the rest of his direct family wished him to have a Greek Orthodox service. It was a difficult time for this family as they negotiated their way not only through the passing of a loved one, but in fulfilling his wishes.

In turn, there was some conflict and hurt amongst the families for this reason. We all worked together, and I must commend his wife and daughter who truly wanted to carry out the wishes of their father, whilst pleasing his family. We were able, in this case, to get a special dispensation and have a Greek Priest join us for the first part of the civil service. Whilst not everyone was happy with this, it was the best way to get through this situation.

At the time of a loved one's passing, often emotions are heightened. It can be a very difficult and upsetting time for all involved. I often think of this family and of their willingness to please all parties concerned. I am so proud of how they handled the situation at this time.

Statistics in Australia show that one in three marriages now end in divorce. In the United States, about forty to fifty percent of married couples divorce. The divorce rate for subsequent marriages is even higher. With these high statistics, it is no wonder that in the work I do, I see blended families who are there to say farewell to a loved one. Often there is conflict. However, often I am blown away by the deep respect and care these two blended families have for one another and how they come together on the day to pay tribute, whilst respecting the other one's wishes.

One such family I met in 2017. Their husband and father, Norman, was eighty one years old when he passed. There were so many incredible stories I heard about his life but one I thought I would share was when he was a Coldstream Guard at Buckingham Palace. The family shared with me some remarkable photos of Normie at the age of eighteen years, dressed in uniform, protecting the Queen. He shared many stories of sneaking Princess Margaret back into the Palace so that the Queen Mother didn't know. Remarkable stories! Normie was immensely proud of his history in being a Guard at Buckingham Palace as was his family. How many people can say they were a Guard for the Queen? And his dear little grand-daughter Charlotte asked her grandmother Karen just before the funeral if the Queen would be there today.

What struck me about the family, whilst meeting them, above all else was how respectful of one another they were. Normie had two daughters, and remarried later in life and became a step-father as well. Throughout the preparations for this service it was so evident to me the care and respect the daughters had for Normie's second wife, and vice versa. This has showed me that blended families can also have incredibly loving, caring relationships as well. It was such a beautiful lesson for me to learn. As I am now a single mother, it gave me hope that one day I too will have the same. There doesn't have to be dysfunction in blended families.

This next story I will share taught me many lessons. Colin was only forty nine years old when he passed. He had only separated three months prior from his wife when he suddenly passed away. Grief is all the more different when it is a sudden passing and you find family members not only in complete shock but utter turmoil. This was a service where there was high conflict, heightened because of the recent marriage separation, as well as the sudden death of their son, their husband and their father. It saddens me to see people in such pain, turmoil and conflict. When I met with some family members, I had been warned there may be some conflict. I am happy to say there was no conflict that I witnessed at all. I saw a family coping as best they could under such a difficult situation. Whilst I am sure there was blame and judgment, that was never ever shown to me.

On the day of the service it was highly emotional. This death seemed so needless. A loss of a life. I couldn't help but notice, however, the conflict amongst the room. His ex-wife and daughters were on one side of the room. His mother and father and siblings, on the other. All I can do in this case is be there for all of them. His father and mother sat alone, at the front of the chapel. When his father got up to deliver his eulogy, I went and sat with his wife and held her hand as she was all alone. I couldn't help but think how it must have felt for her to have been saying goodbye to her son. As a mother to a mother, I could not even fathom the pain she would have been going through.

I commend the family on how they were during this service. As difficult a time as it was, and as much conflict as there had been, there was total peace in that room for their son, husband and father. They were all there to pay their last respects to Colin, and they certainly did that.

Dysfunction comes in all shapes and sizes. What I am most proud of is on the day when it counts the most, the families can come together to say their final goodbyes. There is always a time in the service where I feel complete and utter peace. I feel the whole congregation of people come together as one. It is an overwhelming experience for me, particularly when there is so much conflict. I cannot help but think there is another presence in that room at that point in time, shining love and light, peace and healing upon everyone.

Sometimes I feel the moment they leave the room and go to the lounge area for refreshments they are back in turmoil and conflict. Other times I feel the peace. It is my hope that peace remains over the families for a long time to come.

Quite possibly the service which stands out the most for me is this one. Not for happy reasons either. Rather, it was a very sad situation, on many counts. A man had passed away who was in his eighties, with many regrets and only one friend supporting him. There was a lot of dysfunction within his life, and even at his funeral. It was a sad day for everyone involved.

This man had made choices in his life of which many did not approve. He had several children yet at the time of his passing he was only in contact with one of them. This man had made decisions in his life that hurt many people.

I was called to conduct this funeral. There were three different parties I was dealing with, at war with one another. It is a difficult task to write a service that they are all happy with, but I got about to work. I saw this as my way of being of service, to bring as much peace as possible into their lives. I saw it as my way also of helping a man who at the time of his death, had many regrets. In his final months, he knew he had done harm to those around him. I came in with no judgment, rather compassion for him and for all of the family members around me.

7 Life Lessons Learned Through Loss

I will not lie. This was one of the most difficult of circumstances and was a very difficult service to do. At one stage during one of the speeches, someone stood up, used some profanity, and left. I did not take it personally rather I saw it as someone hurting badly. When we moved to the cemetery for the burial, you could have cut the air with a knife. It was dysfunction at its extreme. It was sad to know that the actions of one person, had such a massive impact on the lives of so many.

My lesson here is whilst we should live each day like it's our last, we also need to consider how our actions affect loved ones around us. How our actions affect the lives of those we are leaving behind. This man's actions had a massive impact in so many ways. Some of his children were there as a way of closure for someone who caused them so much pain. Some of the children were there to make peace with his actions. Some of his children were there as a way of acceptance with their half brothers and sisters. Some were there to grieve someone they loved so dearly. Some were there to say good riddance. I am sorry if that sounds harsh, but that is the truth.

I say this to you to show you that our actions affect

others in so many ways. It is about putting ourselves in someone else's shoes and feeling how it felt for them. This day I really didn't know where to look, there was so much pain and angst for so many reasons. There was so much anger. There was so much frustration for a man that chose, what some considered, to be the wrong path.

Whilst dysfunction in families is normal, the point I am wanting to make with this story is your actions can cause great harm. One man's actions caused great dysfunction that affected many people, for the long term. How does one get over that? It is my wish for this whole extended family that in time they will find forgiveness and peace within their own hearts. Our actions and the way we choose to live our lives has great impact on others. The saddest part is that this man knew in the end he had hurt a great many people, however, he felt it was too late to make amends.

If I look back on my own story with my own family, had I not taken the courage to make amends with my parents, it may never have happened. For so long I had not contacted them, because of fear and let's be honest, because of hurt. Had I not learnt my life lessons through this work, who knows how long it would have been before I had made contact. Maybe it would have been at my own father's funeral and, by then, too late. I would have had deep regrets if that was the case.

What I witnessed at this man's funeral, I couldn't help but wonder why he did not contact his family in his final months, or better still, to make amends? Was it pride? Was it stubbornness? Was it regret? What if he did? Would it have made a difference to his family members? Would they now be carrying their lives out differently? Would they be more at peace?

Our actions certainly do account for plenty.

The final story I wish to share with you about dysfunction in families is another personal one for me.

As a divorced single parent of two young boys, I won't lie, it hasn't always been easy whilst navigating a *new* relationship with my boy's father. There had been betrayal involved, and my heart had well and truly been broken. In the three years since it ended, it has been tender and difficult at times. We both love our children and want the best for them. We do our best to communicate regarding their needs, however, it has at times been hard to do when there has been so much hurt and anger.

I learned a valuable lesson from a family I met with recently and one I am forever grateful for as it will have a huge impact on my children's lives forever more. The father, Kevin, passed away suddenly in his mid-sixties leaving behind his two twin boys in their early thirties. It was a devastating time for the families. In the following days when I was to meet with them, their grief was evident. The boys' mother, Mary, was also present. Even though Mary and Kevin had been divorced for a number of years, they had always maintained an amicable relationship for their children. If there was ever a time these boys needed their Mum's support, it was now.

Mary was a pillar of strength for her boys; grieving the sudden loss of their father, all the while no doubt navigating her own personal grief of losing a person who fathered her children and whom she had spent a large portion of her life with. Grief is grief and whether you are separated or divorced, you feel something.

What struck me about Mary was the love she had for her boys. She wanted to take their pain away and make this easier for them. She had written many notes to give to me to help me with preparing the eulogy and the service for their father. It was evident that Mary still had a relationship with her ex-husband's brothers and sisters as well and they were calling in to check on one another.

It was evident from stories relayed to me, that Kevin's boys were the light of his life. They were his everything. He would often say being a father was the best thing that ever happened to him. Everything he did, he did for his boys.

Whilst sitting with her and the boys, Mary shared something with me that took my breath away. She told me that ever since they separated, every single Mother's Day, Kevin sent her flowers and a card. And he always wrote the same thing, *"Thank you for giving me my greatest gift - my sons."*

Mary told me he has never ever missed a Mother's Day. That is gratitude at its finest. I am sure this couple would have been like other couples navigating a separation and divorce with children involved. It would have been hard. You don't go into a marriage or having children lightly. You dream of spending a happy, long life with your loved one. I am sure the end of their marriage would have been difficult for all involved. Yet somehow, Kevin found gratitude. Despite what had happened in the past, he had gratitude to her and for his sons.

Mary was humble. She wanted no mention of her in the eulogy apart from a family holiday they had all together. She wanted no recognition for having organized it. She just wanted to be the support to her two sons. There was no animosity, no angry thoughts, no nothing. I guess I could say Mary and Kevin's feelings towards each other, in divorce, could put mine and many others to shame.

My greatest lesson in this, in observing Mary on the day of the funeral was she was there fully for her two boys. Kevin and Mary's respect for one another, even in death, was so evident.

It got me thinking - if something happened to my boys' father, how would it be for them? Of course, I would be there for them. Of course, I would support them. But is it amicable with his family? No. Could I sit with the boys and prepare his funeral with no animosity from his family? At this point in time, I would honestly say, no. My boys deserve better than that.

Had I ever expressed gratitude to the boys' father since

our separation, on him giving me without a doubt my greatest gifts of all? No. Will I? Now having learnt this lesson? Absolutely. Yes.

Yes, I have been hurt and betrayed. Yes, I have endured more than what I should have had to. But my love for my children is far greater and they deserve better. I do not want to show them dysfunction. I want to show them gratitude. I want to show them that love still exists between myself and their father. Not the love that once was there, but love in another way now. It's the shared love of our boys. It's shown through gratitude of one another for giving each other our greatest gift. And it starts with me. If I want to instil this change, it must come from within.

As I delivered the service, I observed Kevin's two boys sitting at the front of the service with their mother sitting in between them. I watched one son as a pall-bearer, carry his father's coffin to his final resting place, whilst the other walked arm-in-arm with his mother. Breathtakingly beautiful. I decided I will change, for my boys.

The next Father's Day, I sent my ex-husband a card. It said:

Sharon Muscet

"Happy Father's Day. Thank you for giving me my greatest gift – our boys."

Because he did. And I am so grateful. That day I felt a sense of forgiveness and acceptance wash over me. I made a vow to myself every Father's Day forevermore, to always send my boys' father a card expressing my thanks to him. I cannot begin to tell you how this one act has had a profound effect on the relationships with my ex-husband already and in turn has had a positive effect on the way we parent our children. Rather than focus on the hurt and the past, it is now about focusing on the present – on our gifts – our boys - and their future.

For me I chose to put my dysfunctional relationship aside, and find forgiveness, and acceptance. It wasn't that I just woke up and thought - I am going to feel grateful for him today.

I acknowledge that every story of dysfunction in families is different. The purpose of this life lesson for me was firstly, to learn that dysfunction is normal in families and there is nothing to feel ashamed about. Through my experiences in dealing with hundreds of families, I have been given privileged insight into all the different types of family dynamics and many points of view.

What you do with this life lesson is up to you, however, I wish you to consider the following:

Is there dysfunction within your family, or those closest to you? If so, is it something that can be resolved? How would you feel knowing that loved person you are in conflict with has passed away? Would you have any regrets?

My advice is, if there is even a slither of regret, then you need to do something about it. Make contact. Wipe the slate clean. Come from a place of forgiveness. Forgiveness in others is one of our greatest virtues. It took me a long time to get my head around forgiveness. Forgiveness is not saying, "it's okay that you treated me badly." Forgiveness is saying that you no longer wish to carry that pain or hurt, and you are choosing to get on with your life. It doesn't mean that you are accepting fault with what has been done to you. Forgiveness is saying that you are choosing to now release those feelings and feel free.

Sharon Muscet

I cannot tell you what this lesson has done for me. Lifting the shame. The feeling of peace and freedom I now have. There are healthy boundaries in place in my relationship with my family. I have been able to find forgiveness and acceptance and in turn gratitude for my greatest gifts – my boys. This has had a big impact on my children's lives already. Mostly, however, it has had a big impact on mine and the way I choose to live my life.

My life lesson is this:

Dysfunction with loved ones does happen. It is a part of life.

It is how you choose to deal with it that is the real key to all of this.

If your dysfunction is hurting you, rather than bringing you peace, then it is up to you to do something about it, for it is you who is the one being hurt the most.

Once our loved ones have passed on, we cannot turn back the clock. You need to decide whether you will have regrets after they have gone.

My wish is for you to be at peace with whatever it is that you decide.

7 Life Lessons Learned Through Loss

I have recorded a video to inspire and support you. To learn more about this valuable life lesson, please visit my website -

www.sharonmuscet.com/resources/videos/7lifelessons/

Life Lesson 5:

Be of service to others

7 Life Lessons Learned Through Loss

One of my greatest life lessons I have learned in the work that I do, is this: be of service to others. There is always someone going through something more than you. This lesson is about standing in someone else's shoes, despite what is going on for you, and truly being there for another person.

We all have *stuff* going on in our lives. We are all consumed in our fast-paced world. We are all consumed with social media, and at times I wonder whether we have lost the art of truly connecting with another person. The words *'are you okay?'* to another person may seem meaningful when asked, but do people actually listen to the answer? Do people even want to know the answer?

Recently, I was going through a difficult time. I shared this with a group of friends. It was the first time I had been vulnerable and shared with this particular group what was going on for me at the time. One of the ladies responded, *"Oh, Sharon, we are all going through something, get over it."* Those words upset me at the time. It made me question firstly, the friendship, and secondly, do people actually want to know what another is feeling? Have we lost that art of truly being there for another person and connecting?

However, I flipped my way of thinking. It made me think of this friend who was so quick to shut me down at a time when I was needing her. I stood in her shoes. I thought about what she was going through and realised, that she too was hurting. She was going through a difficult time herself. Perhaps she wasn't in the headspace to think of me and what I was dealing with.

I cannot tell you the number of times when my work, meeting with grieving families, writing a service and then delivering it, has helped me. Let me explain.

There were many times when all seemed lost in my world – with the sudden ending of my marriage. My whole world, for a time, caved in. My boys and I were forced to leave our home, and I found myself in a brand-new world. It was a devastating time and for the next two years I set about rebuilding our lives.

There were many days I didn't want to get out of bed but I did for the sake of my boys. It is what kept me going, as did my funeral celebrancy work and the families which brought it all into perspective.

I conduct approximately five funerals a week. I am self-employed and work with more than twenty different funeral homes across the city in which I live. I work with about thirty different Funeral Directors. These people I work with are all extraordinary people. They have one of the toughest jobs in the world. Yet you ask them, and they would tell you it is the most rewarding job in the world. They see it all, they can be the one on the scene as soon as a loved one has departed. They are at the family homes seeing hearts break. They are with the families when the bodies are removed from the home. They are there and have to deal with conflict within families as well. They have some of the best negotiation skills I have seen, and I have worked all around the world in executive positions.

What I am most impressed with is their ability to match a family with the right Funeral Celebrant. They don't just call any celebrant. It has to be the right fit for the family. The family would share whether they want a religious service or a civil service. Then they would express whether they wish for a female or a male celebrant. Then they would be asked what type of service they are looking for. In my case, the Funeral Directors know my services are a *Celebration of Life*. They know the work that I do. They know I weave a person's personal story into my service.

Sharon Muscet

I pride myself very much on my work. Knowing that I can make a difference to a family, in some small way, at the most difficult time in their life, is why I do what I do. It is what makes it the most rewarding.

It has been my funeral celebrancy work that has kept me going through my most difficult times. Every time I get a call from a Funeral Director, no matter what is going on in my life, I will always be there for that family. They need me. They need me to represent their loved one in the best possible light. The family need to feel confident in knowing the send-off for their loved one is going to be incredible.

I have had moments when it felt like my world was crashing in, and then I get a call. It could be a ninety year old man, or a sixty five year old woman, or a six year old girl or a three day old baby who has passed away. Suddenly, it puts everything into perspective for me.

When we can truly be of service to others, that is the greatest of gifts we can give. When you can truly stand in someone else's shoes and be there for that person, one hundred percent. The best way for any of us to work through what it is that is going on in our own lives, is to be there for someone else. Show love, kindness, compassion, empathy - listen, and connect.

Whenever I feel that something in my life is not going the way it should, I think of what others are going through. I know that there is always someone else out there going through something more.

Most importantly, at the time when something in your life is not going the way you feel it should, go out and be of service to someone else. Whether that is looking after your children, your parents, just being there for a friend. Whether it is that you go and do some charity work, do that extra bit for your employer. Whatever, it doesn't matter. The thing is to go out and be of service. The moment you step outside of your own shoes and can be there for someone else in their time of need, is the greatest of healings for you.

There have been times, when I have been standing up at a funeral service, it could be in front of ten people or three hundred people; the feeling is always the same. I am here of service. I am here to make a difference. I am here to share peace amongst these people. My own world seems so much brighter. My own world doesn't seem so sad any more. I know that within my own world everything is going to be okay. In my own world the problem doesn't even seem as relevant anymore. That is because I know that there is someone else out there going through something so much more than me. I know that I am here to be of service to those people. That makes me feel worthy. That makes me feel valuable.

I believe we are all put here on this earth to be of service to other people. Our own true happiness lies when we can be there for others. Really be there.

A lot of people ask me, "*How do you not get sad when you do these services?*" or "*How do you not cry? I would be terrible if I did something like that.*" Others have said, "*You must have a heart of steel to be able to stand at a child's funeral and not feel anything.*"

The thing is, I feel everything. I feel more than most would at that particular time. I have a big, kind heart and am the biggest softie that ever walked. Again, it is not about me. As soon as you say, "*I would never be able to do that*" or "*I would just cry,*" you are making it all about you. This is not what this is about. I take myself out of the equation, I take my feelings outside. My feelings are irrelevant. What is relevant is how I can be of service to this family and how I can best represent their loved one who has passed.

It is removing judgment from situations. It is removing my own sadness, my own grief, my own thoughts on the situation. I am here to be of service. I am here to shine light and love, peace and healing on them. The best way I can describe it is I go into a completely different mode when I am there, I deliver the service, whilst being of service.

It is only after the service, whilst the families are placing floral tributes on the coffin and walking out, that I let my guard down. I am standing in the families' shoes, watching their hearts break. It is then, that if you look closely at me, you will always see tears in my eyes. For that is when I allow myself, to truly feel those feelings.

Knowing you can be there for others, knowing there is always someone else going through something more than you, and being of service, is one of the keys to your own healing and happiness. I wanted to share a story of how I have seen many people overcome their own loss. Again, it is all to do with being of service.

I met with two lovely ladies who had recently lost their

mother named June, at the age of eighty seven. Oh, how they adored their mother. June had lost her husband twenty four years earlier and as you could expect, she found life very difficult adjusting to this loss. She was a gentle and kind lady, who was also known as a social butterfly. She was always one to strike up conversations with people at shopping centres or whilst out at lunch.

It was not long after losing her husband, that she struck up a conversation with a young man at a bus stop. She learned that he was an international student and was looking for somewhere to live. June, being quite lonely in her home on her own, took to inviting him to come and live with her for company. The family shared with me that initially they were concerned when their mother phoned them to tell them what she had just done. However, they soon discovered that having international students live with her was to be the best thing that could have happened for her.

She later went on to invite a Japanese girl to live with her. Many years later, this girl's family paid for June to travel to Japan for her wedding. This became a highlight of June's life. June wore a traditional Japanese dress for the wedding. She loved this dress so much that the family chose it for June to wear when she was laid to rest.

June also had a Taiwanese student live with her for a while. His family, knowing she was finding life hard since the passing of her husband, invited her to Taiwan to visit. They were wonderful to her and it aided tremendously in her healing. She loved this family and they looked after her. The family showed me a photo of June in Taiwan, riding on the back of a motorbike. She was so happy. She went back there at various times over the next three to four years.

June developed a love for all things oriental. She took up Tai-Chi, enjoyed travel and went on to have many trips to Japan, Taiwan and China. Even in her seventies she backpacked with students in hostels, it was good for her and she saw different parts of the world.

At June's funeral, her first international student to live with her was present with his wife. He spoke so beautifully of June and his words were touching. He spoke of the impact June had on his life. He told us of the day they met at the bus stop. He said he was in a sad and difficult position not having anywhere to live, and he did not know what to do. Suddenly he met June and she changed his life.

June was able to turn her own loss into being a person of service, by housing international students. She became their friend and later she was invited into their families. Her decision in housing international students aided not only in her own healing but changed this man's life. Her initial act of service, resulted in a flow on effect that impacted so many others.

June's story is a true story of how being of service can aid not only in your own healing, but also impact someone else's life. It is a truly remarkable example of how one lady overcame her loss by being of service.

I see and hear of people being of service every single day to those who are unwell, as well as to the elderly. In this line of work, I hear of the wonderful nurses, palliative care nurses, doctors, aged care homes, and carers, to name a few. I have heard of many family members who put their lives on hold to care for their sick or elderly loved one until their passing. I see unconditional love and I see being of service at its very best.

Yvonne was eighty four years old when she passed away. Her elderly son Greg had put his life on hold for the last ten years to live and look after his Mum. I recall on the day of her service how his brother and sister paid tribute to Greg and expressed their absolute gratitude for all he had done for her. They acknowledged how big a job it was for him to be her carer. They saw how fastidious he was. He loved and cared for their Mum unconditionally and words could not express from them, to him, how wonderful he was in caring for her for the last ten years. John, his brother, mentioned if this was the Olympics, he deserved a Gold medal for every day that he cared for her.

On a recent flight to America, I sat next to a lovely lady. She tearfully shared with me how her sister had passed away six weeks earlier and she had been her carer. She was travelling to America to visit friends and have some time away. She felt very tired, understandably.

It reminded me of how many family carers I meet in the line of work that I do. I meet them after their loved one has passed away. I led a service recently for a lady who had just turned one hundred years when she passed. Her daughter had been her carer for many years prior to her passing. I recall speaking to her, and seeing her on the day of the service. She was exhausted. She was in much need of a rest. She had sacrificed her life and so much of her time to care for her mother. She did it out of love, duty and obligation.

It dawned on me that day not only what a large part our carers play in looking after those who are elderly, or unwell, but also how important it is that those carers are able to rest and look after themselves as well. It was a lesson I learned that day. This lady was of true service to her mother, however, almost to the detriment of herself.

I wish to acknowledge all carers and all that they do. Their strength, courage, and most of all their love, is incredible as they care for and are of service to their loved one until their passing.

My life lesson is this:

Know whenever you are going through a tough time in life, there is someone out there going through more, and there is someone you can help.

When you are experiencing any type of loss, being of service will aid not only in your healing but more so it will impact so many other people's lives.

When you are being of service to another, remember to always look after you and ensure you are properly cared for and rested.

Being there for others is, in my opinion, one of the greatest gifts we can ever give. And you know what? That feeling of being there for others in their time of need, is the greatest gift you will ever receive.

I have recorded a video to inspire and support you. To learn more about this valuable life lesson, please visit my website -

www.sharonmuscet.com/resources/videos/7lifelessons/

Sharon Muscet

Life Lesson 6:

Be prepared for your death

Sharon Muscet

7 Life Lessons Learned Through Loss

For too long, in Western society we have seen death as a *taboo topic*. So much fear surrounds it. Why is that? Death is a natural part of life, as natural as birth. Yet, why don't we discuss it? My experience shows it is too painful to go there. It has been my wish in the writing of this book that we turn our fear of death, into love.

It is my wish to create a world-wide movement in the way people view death. I wish for death to be discussed openly with one another, for so many reasons. Being more prepared for death is one of them.

We all have a start date and an end date. What is important is how we fill the blanks in between. It reminds me of a poem called, *The Dash* by Linda Ellis, an excerpt follows:

"I read of a man who stood to speak at a funeral
of a friend.
He referred to the dates on the tombstone from
the beginning...to the end.
He noted that first came the date of birth and spoke
of the following date with tears,

Sharon Muscet

but said what mattered most of all was the
dash between those years.
For that dash represents all the time they spent
alive on earth
and now only those who loved them know
what that little line is worth.
For it matters not, how much we own, the cars ..
the house ... the cash.
What matters is how we lived and loved and how we
spend our dash."

Are you prepared? Do you fear death? Are you comfortable in talking about death with loved ones? Do you have a will? Have you thought about important details for your funeral? Have you discussed this with your loved ones? Do they know your final wishes? Do they know if you wish to be buried or cremated? Have you written your life story? Have you left a legacy for your generations to come?

In my experience professionally, over the last eight years, I have sat with several hundred families grieving the loss of a loved one ranging from birth, right to the age of one hundred and two years old. I have felt and seen first-hand the fear that surrounds death and the devastating effects on people and families when they are not prepared. Nothing is documented, wills are not prepared, no life story is recorded.

In my experience, I see death is feared. I have tried to talk to some of my friends about the work that I do, and they don't want to know about it. They think if they discuss it with me, it will bring about death of either themselves or a loved one. They think what I do is morbid. They don't understand that for me, this is the most rewarding job I have ever done. It is not even a job for me. It is my calling. It is my purpose. I have worked in corporate, I have earned six figure incomes, I have won world-wide awards in my other business, yet nothing compares to the work that I do here or fulfils me in the same way.

I have spoken with people who, even though in their seventies, still do not have a will. Upon asking them this question, however, the answer is almost always the same. Their answer stems from *fear*.

Many have told me, they believe if they have a will drawn up, they will die. It's as simple as that. I'm not sure whether they realise (and most probably not as it's too painful a thought to consider) the outcome of not having a will. If you pass away without a will, you die *intestate*. Each State in Australia has its own laws about intestacy, however, without a will, you risk your assets being distributed differently to how you would have intended. So why not draw up a will? It is such a simple thing to do. Yet, it seems their fear of dying is just too great.

I have also spoken to many people who are still working in their seventies. They are too afraid to retire as they have seen many of their friends retire and die shortly after, and, feel that this too will happen to them. So, what are they doing? They are working their life away. Not enjoying the fruits of their labour. Once again, they too are living a life based on fear. It seems that they are choosing to make a choice about their life.

I cannot begin to tell you the number of times I have met with families who are in turmoil after the death of their loved one. Not only is there no will, but nothing has been prepared or documented. Already they are grieving the death, now there is extra stress to deal with as well, in regards to their estate and the planning of their funeral.

It surprises me that many of these families lost loved ones due to a terminal illness. In many cases, they did have some time knowing their loved one's outcome. Yet they did not want to discuss the inevitable together. The pain was too great. The fear of the unknown stopped them.

What I find the saddest is that the person has not recorded their life story, so that family have lost the loved one's history, their loved one's culture and their loved ones values. There is now no history to pass onto their loved ones. There is in many cases, no legacy left for generations to come.

What I have found is that, if we as a society start to talk about death, it will eliminate the fear that surrounds it and people will become better prepared for *the last experience of their life.*

One lady who I was inspired by was so incredibly prepared for her passing. She was eighty-seven years old and had planned for her departure for over a decade. Her husband had passed years earlier and she had one son. When I met him, he showed me all of her documentation. I could not believe how prepared she was, more so than anyone I had done a service for before. She was a highly organised person and this ensured that all of her wishes were carried out on the day. Most importantly, this also reduced the stress for the son, as he was already going through his own grieving of having lost her.

She had pre-planned her funeral right up to meeting the Funeral Director beforehand and organized all of her arrangements. She had picked out her coffin, flowers, music and hymns. To make things easier for me in organizing the service, she had also chosen all of her poems and had actually written her entire life story. There is nothing more remarkable than having someone put pen to paper and reading their exact words, handwritten by them.

She had a great love of collecting photos and her son showed me the many boxes that she had kept, all highly organized as well. Her family was her pride and joy, and his was evident with so many family photos placed around the house.

Her son had been her carer for over eight years and the way he spoke so wonderfully of his mother showed me how truly loved and cared for she was. It was beautiful to see. As sad as this time was for her son, I know that having been so organized with her will and estate, and with the whole planning of her funeral, it was easier for him to not only celebrate her life, but also for the healing process for him to begin.

Time and time again I see families completely overwhelmed in the lead up to a funeral. They are meeting with Funeral Directors, Solicitors, having to sort bank details, and often they are running around not really knowing what to do. They are completely exhausted by the time the funeral comes around. I know they often are looking forward to it being over, so they too can start their healing journey.

For me it's about making life that little bit easier for others. It's about taking responsibility for your own life and not expecting other people to sort it for you. It's also about having the send-off that you want – the music, the flowers, the people.

I recently did a service for a forty seven year old woman. She had known she was unwell for the previous eleven months, and was incredibly organized. As I met and sat with her husband and parents to prepare for the service, I recall her husband's remarks to me. He said that, *"they are feeling quite relaxed about it all."* He said they are her *messengers*. She was incredibly organized and he, her Mum and Dad, were carrying out her wishes. He felt there wasn't much thinking for them to do. This is in stark contrast to what I mostly see where families feel very stressed about it all.

She had wound up her business, she had sorted out personal details. She had known what coffin she wanted, the music to play. She had wanted a private service and had written the list of exactly the people she wanted present at her service. These were the people closest to her and she wanted them to know that. It was such an incredibly intimate service. The tributes were outstanding. This was one that will stay with me for such a long time. I think a large part of that is because it was exactly how she wanted it. She was prepared for her death and in turn it made it easier on her family.

Another lady who comes to mind in terms of being prepared was ninety one years old when she passed. She had actually planned her funeral eighteen years before including choosing her music, poems and writing her life story, which she added to over the years. It was such a personal service and it gave the family so much peace knowing the service was exactly how she wanted it.

As I met with her entire family, her grandson summed it up perfectly when he said, *"Nan has saved the day once again – she is still here helping to make our life easier."*

Getting Started

I actually have heard and researched a pilot program in the United States where they ran *Death Education* lessons for high school students. It is a bit like the Sex Education lessons rolled out across many schools for teenagers. This was designed to help children talk openly and feel comfortable in talking about sex. They could ask questions and become better educated. After all it is a part of life. In the case of the Death Education classes, not only did they talk about death, it also got students preparing for death in terms of their parents and grandparents as well. The take on this pilot program was if you start to educate children in schools about death, then we will eventually eliminate the stigma attached to death that it is not something we talk about. I thought it was genius.

There is currently debate in Australia, and in particular in Queensland, about whether Death Education should be taught in classrooms to demystify aging and dying amongst younger Australians. Not only would it help students be more capable of making informed choices when the time comes, but it would also assist young people to become more resilient about loss, ageing, dying and grief.

Apart from the discussed fear that appears to hold many people back, it is also a case of people may not know how to or where to go. If it seems too overwhelming, it is easier to do nothing and put it off for another day. This is why I have prepared some resources and something to help get you started in your journey.

Free templates are available for you to download from my website - www.sharonmuscet.com/resources/free-information

Finally, here is a checklist should you wish to use this book as your resource. This simple checklist will get you started and on your way.

Your Will

- Have an updated will to determine who will get your assets when you pass
- This should be kept with your Power of Attorney (see below) and Advanced Directive (see below)
- People who should have a copy: You, Lawyer, Power of Attorney

Designate Power of Attorney (when necessary)

- Give someone the power to make financial decisions for you, when you are not able to make those decisions for yourself. For example becoming incapacitated due to an accident
- People who should have a copy: You, Lawyer, Power of Attorney

Fill out Advanced Directive

- Designates your medical wishes
- People who should have a copy: You, Doctor, Power of Attorney

Prepare a Contact List

- ☐ People who should be immediately notified of the death (immediate family, Power of Attorney, etc)
- ☐ Those who should be notified and invited to the funeral/memorial service
- ☐ People who you DO NOT want notified and who are NOT to attend the funeral/ memorial service

Plan and Document Funeral Wishes

- ☐ What type of service you would like – religious or civil?
- ☐ Where you want the service i.e. chapel, church, beach, park?
- ☐ Burial, Cremation, Donation to Science?
- ☐ Where you want to be buried/cremated
- ☐ What sort of coffin do you want?

- ☐ Investigate pre-paid option plan – Funeral Homes offer these
- ☐ Which Funeral company do you prefer?
- ☐ What sort of music would you like?
- ☐ What flowers would you like?
- ☐ Is there a theme you would like on the day i.e. would you like everyone to wear a colour?

Write your Life Story

- ☐ Allows you to decide what is written and read at your service. This will leave a legacy for generations to come

Make a list of important account information

- ☐ All accounts so they can be closed after your death
- ☐ Bank details
- ☐ Utilities
- ☐ Internet
- ☐ Mobile Phone

- ☐ Passwords i.e. for bank accounts, insurances, Facebook, other social media

Make a list of death benefits & insurance policies
- ☐ Car insurance
- ☐ Home insurance
- ☐ Life insurance
- ☐ Superannuation
- ☐ Centrelink/Social Security

Make a list of assets
- ☐ Titles
- ☐ Registrations

Like I stated at the start, death is a natural process of life. It is as natural as birth. We all prepare for the birth of our babies with great detail. It is important for us to prepare for our death in advance. Whether our death is expected or not, it is up to us to prepare. This will not only create a peace-filled end of your life, but also relieve those family members whom have been left behind.

7 Life Lessons Learned Through Loss

It really is important to start your checklist today. Don't let it overwhelm you. It will take some time and energy to complete. It is so much better if you take the time now to prepare for your death. In turn, your passing when the time arrives, will be peaceful, for both you, your family and friends.

My life lesson is this:

Our life is like a candle that flickers, a reminder that life is as fragile as the flickering light. It is a reminder that in reality, we are nothing but a breath away from death. Be prepared for your Death.

Planning for your own death—whether it is expected or not—can take time and energy to complete. Start now. It is much better to take the time now, while you have it, to lay out your plans, wishes, directions and desires, so your passing will be peaceful, for both you, your family and friends.

It is after all, the last experience of your life and one of the most important experiences of your life, as well.

Sharon Muscet

I have recorded a video to inspire and support you. To learn more about this valuable life lesson, please visit my website -

www.sharonmuscet.com/resources/videos/7lifelessons/

Life Lesson 7:

Leave your legacy - record your life story

Sharon Muscet

7 Life Lessons Learned Through Loss

You have now read six of the life lessons learned through loss. Hopefully it has given you some new found thought processes on how to live your best life. Tools such as deciding how you want to be remembered. There are so many stories on love to inspire you to live a better life. There are stories on gratitude, on how to be there for other people and building your Tribe. All of these lessons are there to culminate in you living your best life.

Now that you have read and understood these lessons, and are putting into practice ways to live your best life, my seventh final lesson, I feel, is so important. It is now time to record your life story, for you to leave a legacy for generations to come. It is each of our responsibility to leave this for our family and loved ones.

Let's think practically again. What would be the five key points that you would include in your life story? What do you consider to be the meaning and purpose of your life? How do you want to be remembered? What do you want to be remembered for? What is it you want people to say about you when you are no longer here?

Have you ever shared your life story with your family? Would they know things such as:

- Your fondest childhood memory?
- Your greatest achievement?
- Your first love?
- Your biggest hurt?
- Your deepest regret?
- Your contribution made to society?
- Your biggest learning in life so far?

My Life Story

I have found that, in the eight years I have worked as a Funeral Celebrant, there is something we all have in common. What I know for sure is, *Every life has a meaning and a purpose. Every single person has a story inside them.*

However, of the families I have met, I have also discovered this: *In most cases, families do not know their loved one's life story.*

In all but several cases, no life story (or eulogy) has been prepared, or documented by the person themselves. It is left to the families, whilst grieving, to remember relevant facts and stories, in helping me to deliver the celebration of their life.

This got me thinking, w*hy is that? Why do we not record our life story? Why do we not share our life stories with our families? Why are we not asking them about theirs?*

Research tells us that there is a history of storytelling within Tribes. Tribes such as the Native Americans and the Indigenous community, all used storytelling - through word, dance and drawings - as a way to preserve their culture, whilst educating in the history and traditional values of their people.

For the Native Americans, oral storytelling traditions allowed Tribes to transmit their understandings of themselves and their worlds to their children and their children's children. This all but guaranteed that members of each Tribe would never forget their roots or lose sight of important knowledge that would allow them to exist.

In the Indigenous community, the role of the storyteller was to preserve their culture, whilst educating in the history and traditional values of their people.

Have we, as a society, lost this art of storytelling within

our own Tribes? Are we losing our history, culture and values? Are we no longer leaving that knowledge for generations to come?

I will share with you a part of my life story when I almost died. I had a freak accident when I was thirty-three. I stepped on the tail of a sting ray. I was off my feet for two years, fighting to save the use of my left foot and toes being amputated. I had ten operations and had a permanent PICC line inserted into my arm for a long time. The toxins caused great damage to my vital organs. It was a heart attack that saw me look death straight in the eye.

It was Easter Sunday. I was at home. I had woken with the most intense pain in my chest right up to my jaw. The pain was indescribable. An ambulance was called. The paramedics performed an ECG on me. I saw the ambulance officer's glance between one another when they read my ECG. It was the look they gave each other that told me everything. I was scared. I was close to dying and I knew it. My children were huddled in a corner. They too were scared at what they saw happening to their Mummy.

When I arrived at the hospital, a team of doctors including an emergency heart surgeon, met me and he said,

"*Sharon, you have had a heart attack.*" The only words I could muster up to say to him were, "*No shit!*" (Quite funny when I look back at this, but at the time however it was not!).

At this particular time, all I could think of were my boys. *Was this how I wanted them to have last seen me? How will they remember me? How do I want to be remembered?* These three questions went over and over in my mind, at a time that was quite possibly the most vulnerable of my life.

That day I put up the biggest fight of my life, and I survived. A few days after I left hospital, I had gone with my husband at the time, to take our two boys to the playground. I was too weak to get out of the car, so I sat in the car and watched them play. The reality of what had happened had hit me. I felt a deep understanding of how fragile life is, and that we can be taken at any time.

Then it was like this light-bulb came on in my mind, and I had this epiphany. I thought, *If I was meant to be gone, I would be gone. I am alive. I am here for a reason. My life has meaning. My life has purpose. I must record the story of my life.* I thought, *How do I want to be remembered?*

Sharon Muscet

What do I want my boys to know?

It was at that moment I started writing my life story. The words started to flow. In doing this, it helped me uncover the meaning and purpose of my life. I now have a legacy for my two boys, their children, and their children and for generations to come. I read it to my boys, chapter by chapter, like a bedtime story, over and over. They love it.

My children know my hopes, my dreams, my aspirations, my childhood, my hurts, my achievements, my true loves. They know it all. We are now working on theirs together. It has been an incredible journey so far to sit with my two sons and share their own dreams and aspirations, what they see as their greatest achievements, their deepest hurts. It has brought me so much closer to my children. It has become a ritual to sit down and add to our life stories.

It is my wish to leave you inspired to record your own life story. I want to leave you inspired to share it with your family. I want to leave you inspired to ask your family their life story; to sit with them and talk about it.

Time is so precious. Life is so fragile. Your life has meaning and purpose. You are here for a reason. It is up to you to leave this knowledge for your generations to come.

7 Life Lessons Learned Through Loss

Sit down with your families, record their life story so they too leave their legacy. It will bring you closer to them. Get yourself a journal and write it down. Or record it, on video, or on your phone. It can be as simple as that! Sit with your parents or your grandparents and start to ask them questions whilst you record. Questions like:

- What is your fondest childhood memory?
- What would you say is your greatest achievement?
- Who or what was your first love?
- What has been your biggest hurt?
- What has been your deepest regret? Can you fix that whilst you are still here?
- What has your contribution to society been?
- What has been your biggest learning in life so far?

You will be surprised what you hear. You will learn so much more about your loved ones by doing this. You will have a record of it, whether you have written this in a journal or recorded it on video. If you choose to record it on video, you will be able to re-watch it for all of time, long after they have passed. There has been times when families have shown me a video of their loved one after they have passed, just of them singing, talking or smiling, and the joy on their face to relive their loved one over and over again, is priceless. If you record them sharing some of their life story, you will have that to play over and over, as well as pass down the history, culture and values of your loved one to future generations.

Through the writing of my own life story, I discovered the meaning and the purpose of my life. It is to create a movement in the way we view death, and that includes being prepared for death and inspiring people to write their life stories. This movement is called *The Love in Death*. I have visions to create templates, journals, apps, and flash cards so that we get back to the art of story-telling and story-writing with our families - our Tribes.

I ask you, how do you want to be remembered? And I challenge you, right now, to write down five key points for your life story, starting here:

7 Life Lessons Learned Through Loss

Five key points for my life story

☐ _____

_____

☐ _____

_____

☐ _____

_____

☐ _____

_____

☐ _____

_____

The importance of leaving a legacy for your family

I first presented my idea of *The Love in Death* to a group of fifty people in February 2018. Before then, there were very few people that knew of the world-wide movement I wanted to create. It had been an idea that was four years in the making. I had sat on this idea, and each service I did and each lesson I learned, it became clearer and clearer to me that I needed to share this message with the world.

I was unsure what type of reaction I would get from

people, yet I had such a strong desire to get this message out to the world. I have always loved professional speaking, so I booked myself into a course in Sydney, run by international speaker, Sam Cawthorn. I had actually first seen Sam present four years prior, around the same time my ideas for *The Love in Death* were born. I look back and think this book was not ready to be born then, as I was still learning my valuable life lessons from each family that I met, each life that was lost, and each service that I conducted.

The first people I ever presented my ideas to were from the professional speaking program. It was the first time I had ever shared my concept of creating a movement in the way we view death. I shared my story on why it is so important to write your own life story. I received overwhelming words of encouragement from all of the people present.

One lady said I was an *"Angel."* She was from Vietnam and expressed that this message very much needed to be heard in Vietnam. More people needed to start talking openly about death, and recording their life stories. She had been a survivor of the war and she had written an incredible memoir. However, there are not many that have.

One lady shared with me that her mother has Alzheimer's. She no longer has the capacity to remember her daughter, let alone remember any of her own life story. Her daughter shared with me if only she had heard my speech and the importance of recording your life story, before her mother was diagnosed. She is so sad that she no longer has any capacity to hear her mother's life story. It is too late for her.

One man at the course shared with me that he was now inspired to go home and sit with both of his parents and ask them their life story. He had never done that. I was pleased that if anything, this was opening up communication between him and his parents. Learning from one another. He in turn will learn about their life and their legacy.

It is about opening up the lines of communication, learning from one another. Imagine a world if families sit with one another and share their life stories. We live in a fast-paced world where there are work pressures, jam-packed schedules, financial stresses and social media distractions, and, little time to sit around a table to talk with one another.

We have lost the art of story-telling. If we continue, we will lose our history amongst our families. Family values will be lost. I cannot stress how many families I have sat with and asked a simple question like, "*Where did Mum go to school?*" or "*What was your Dad's first job?*" where they are unable to answer. I cannot tell you also how many times I also hear, "*If only I had taken the time to sit down and listen.*"

It is one thing to say you are going to record it, another thing to actually get started. It doesn't have to be a lengthy exercise. It's a matter of starting. In our technological world we live in, you could use your video on your mobile phone or your laptop. Start with asking them a question, "*Where did you grow up?*" or "*What was your childhood like?*" I am sure once prompted with questions, they will be away.

Recording this time together makes it even more special as you will be able to play it back over the years. That video will be around for generations to come. You will have preserved history within your family which is so important.

7 Life Lessons Learned Through Loss

I know that many people can feel overwhelmed in recording their life story. Where to begin? What to write? Many people fear death and are scared of it, so don't want to think about recording their life story. Their families are scared too. They may have a family member dying and they don't know what to do, where to go, how to record their loved-one's life story, or how to prepare. They feel alone.

I am creating a movement so people record their life stories for their families, to keep for generations to come. A gift to leave to your family. I am creating a movement so that people who are facing death, have a place to go to for support so they don't feel so alone.

I provide an on-line community and step-by-step training and support in recording your life story. This ensures your life story lives on within your family for generations to come. This is a community that provides peace of mind so you know that you are not alone. I provide a consulting service for people facing death.

For a free template on recording your life story, plus much more information, visit my website at www.sharonmuscet.com

Sharon Muscet

Life stories I have had the privilege to read

There is no greater privilege for me than to read a life story by the person who has actually put pen to paper. There is something about knowing these words are coming from their heart, from their very essence. They are stating all of the things that are most important to them. Like I said previously, in the several hundred services I have done to date, there have only been a handful where the person has written their own life story. It has been extraordinary. The people present at the funeral have all said the same as well.

Joan's was the first life story I had ever seen written and I had the privilege of delivering. She is the lady I referred to in *Chapter 2 – Decide how you want to be remembered*. Knowing she had put her pen to paper and talked about her ninety six years was incredible. The detail was extraordinary. What she wrote was from the heart. Her family have this to keep forever more.

Beth, the woman discussed in *Chapter 6 – Be Prepared for your death*, had written the most incredible story of her life. She was very close with all of her family. I remember one of her grandchildren saying to me that even though they were so close to her, they never knew so many things about her life, particularly her earlier years. They said they learnt so much from reading her own life story and were so grateful to have had that. They printed off a copy of her life story for all of the grandchildren and great-grandchildren. They now all have a record of her life and they will all be able to pass on her life story to all of their generations. Her legacy lives on.

Another lady, Dorothy, who I mentioned in *Chapter 6 – Be prepared for your death* had also written her life story. It was handwritten which felt all the more special for me when I could read it from the original. She had put her pen to paper at some stage in her life, and these were the very pages passed onto me to read at the service. Her story was incredible as I shared all the trials and tribulations of her life.

Pauline was one of the most recent services that I have done at the time of writing this book. This lady had Parkinson's Disease for the last ten years. She lost her mobility and the ability to speak and communicate. Prior to this happening, she recorded her life story on paper. She wanted to do this for her grandchildren so that they had a memory of her and what she was like before this crippling disease took over her body. She didn't want her grandchildren to just remember her in her wheelchair, paralysed. She wanted them to know of all she had done and achieved throughout her life. She was an extraordinary woman, so full of life. She was a wonderful dancer and singer and performed in comedy acts. Her two grandchildren sat at her funeral service, overwhelmed knowing she had recorded her life story. I felt overwhelmed that this lady had done this for her grandchildren and that they had a record of her and her life.

I am certain this is why I have remembered all of these ladies, because they had recorded their own life story. There was so much more depth to their story. I saw first-hand, how grateful the families were for having their loved one's life story. They have left legacies for their families for lifetimes to come. That person's history, culture and values has been retained forever more.

It is my greatest wish that we all take note and write our own life stories. We truly are here for a reason and a purpose. Every single life has meaning. The saddest thing for me is often I see people in a funeral service. They place the floral tribute on the coffin, and then they go out to the lounge area for refreshments. As soon as I arrive to join them for a cup of tea, they are talking about the weather, the footy or life in general. Don't get me wrong, they were there and had paid their respects and there is no doubt that people grieve.

However, I cannot help but wonder what happens over the years. If that person did not have their life story recorded, would the generations eventually forget about their loved one? Would the things that mattered most to them be forgotten? It is easy to forget details that I am sure would have mattered to that person.

For me personally, I want to leave my children with a legacy. I want them to know all about their mother. I want their children, and their children's children to know all about me too. I want them to know about my nature, the type of person I was, my qualities, my qualifications, my goals, my dreams, my hurts, and my desires. Most of all I want them to know the impact I created in this world and all about my legacy.

This book is a legacy. My impact is in creating a world-wide movement in the way people view death. It is my hope that I will inspire people to talk about death, to dispel the fear around death. To be more prepared in their death. To record their life story so they too can leave legacies for generations to come. That is my greatest legacy to my children and my generations to come. To know I have made a fundamental difference in this word.

Your life does have meaning and purpose and you are here for a reason. It is up to you to record that so that your children, and your generations know the incredible person that you are and the impact you have made in this world.

I have recorded a video to inspire and support you. To learn more about this valuable life lesson, please visit my website -

www.sharonmuscet.com/resources/videos/7lifelessons/

Final Words

Sharon Muscet

7 Life Lessons Learned Through Loss

In 2018, I led a *Celebration of Life* for a beautiful young girl who had lost her life, aged only fifteen. She loved Cherry Blossoms. So, throughout the service I spoke about the Cherry Blossom, and how it related to her life.

The cherry blossom is a small, delicate pink flower produced by the cherry blossom tree. It is a cultural icon, particularly in Japan, China and other Asian countries. Cherry Blossoms are felt with deep respect around the world not just for their overwhelming beauty, but for their enduring expression of life, death and renewal.

The springtime bloom is a lavish spectacle but remarkably brief; after a short time, the flow of the wind takes those beautiful blossoms. The cherry blossom has deep meaning and represents the beauty and the fragility of life. It also signifies *love*.

I dedicated this poem to this young girl as it represented the cherry blossom and its meaning. It is called, '*The Cherry Blossom*' by Cheyenne Raine:

> "*Flutter your wings, as if your branches were swaying*
> *Spread your feathers, like your blooming flowers*
> *Fly your heart out, as your roots go deeper*

Sharon Muscet

Taste sweet nectar, as you thirst your rain
Sing your song, like wind beneath blossoms
Darling, you're the beauty, of a hummingbird
And the stand still, of a cherry blossom."

The cherry blossom's blooming season is powerful, glorious and, sadly, short-lived – a visual reminder that our lives, too, are fleeting. If you turn to the back cover of this book you are now holding, you will see the beautiful cherry blossoms as your own visual reminder.

Time is so precious. Life is so fragile. Like the cherry blossom, may you live your life fully, amongst the wind and amongst great LOVE. Have no fear. If you have lost a loved one to death, focus on your love for them – *The Love in Death*.

Decide how you want to be remembered in this world and go out and do just that. Love your loved ones. Tell them every day. Live your best life and create impact in this world. Live your life full of gratitude. Know it's not the material things that matter in the end.

Have no regrets. If there is dysfunction with a loved one and you feel there may be regret, fix it. Be of service to others, for that is where you will find fulfilment. Prepare for your final days, it will mean more to your family than you realise. Most importantly, record your life story. Your life has meaning and purpose. You are here for a reason. You have an incredible story inside of you that the world needs to hear. Leave your legacy for your generations to come.

Love life! Love every day you are here on this earth. Be the love you wish to receive. Be the most extraordinary love story that has ever been told.

I hope these *7 Life Lessons Learned Through Loss* have inspired you, transformed you and encouraged you to leave your legacy in this world. May your future be bursting with new possibilities. It has been my privilege to share these powerful and moving stories with you, and for you to get to know my personal story about how these lessons have changed my life. The stories were raw, honest, and from my heart to yours.

I know only too well the fragility of life, personally and professionally. I know that there is a LOVE out there more powerful than any of us could ever believe possible.

Sharon Muscet

Live your life, have no fear, and LOVE. That is my greatest wish for you.

Acknowledgements

To the several hundred people who I have had the privilege to conduct their *Celebration of Life*. Each of their lives profoundly impacted me. Without their life and ending, I would not have learnt these valuable lessons to share with the world. I am eternally grateful for you and your life.

To their families who I spent valuable time with, you were their messengers. You poured your hearts out to me and shared with me your LOVE so I could become the messenger.

To the Funeral Directors and Funeral Assistants who have trusted me in leading services for them and representing their company. I have never met more compassionate people who are of service to families.

Sharon Muscet

To my two sons, Luka and Hugo, thank you for choosing me to be your Mum. I am the luckiest person alive. You two have been my greatest teachers. I know you watch on while I work with families, wrote this book, and founded a global movement. You smother me in kisses and cuddles all the while. You have the biggest, kindest and most empathetic hearts. You are my angels who watch over me. Thank you for always believing in me and loving me.

Thank you to my twin brother, Steve, for your unconditional love and support in everything I have ever done. We rode in on this journey called life together, and you have stood by me every day of my life. I can't express just how much you mean to me. To Nicc, Ellen, Tom and Harry - I love you, and thank you for making my brother so happy.

Thank you, Jennette. You have been my Earth Angel for the last twenty plus years and have been one of the greatest influencers in my life. You helped me find my Spirit. Your love, presence and words are felt always.

Thank you to my Year 11 teacher, Mrs Rundle, you showed me what I could achieve simply by believing in me. I have never forgotten that.

7 Life Lessons Learned Through Loss

To my beautiful friends, Jasmine and Neil, you are family to my boys and I. We adore you. Thank you for always being on the end of the phone Jazzie and with a bottle of champagne waiting when I arrive. To Sarah and Michael, thanks for letting me crash your family gatherings!

To my dear friend Deb, who always has my back and for your unconditional belief and support of me. I love our Thelma and Louise adventures. You are a wonderful person who deserves the best in this life.

My incredible friend Justine, who helped me through one of the toughest times of my life through your unconditional love and support. I will never forget what you did for me. I love our crazy, fun times together.

To Kylie and Sammy, we have been through so many experiences together, and we have always been there for one another. Thank you for being such wonderful friends to me. To Christopher and Paul for being incredible friends also. You are two of the luckiest men alive to have these two girls in your life.

To Sarah (BG), you have been one of my longest-term friends and we have had so many adventures together.

Sharon Muscet

Thank you for our long-lasting friendship built on trust and loyalty, I am so grateful for you.

To Libby, for your absolute belief in me and my message to take to the world. I will never forget what you and Pete have done. I love our Spirit and Angel talks and you just get that about me.

To Andreas, thank you for being a loyal friend to me and always believing in me.

Beautiful Kristen, you are an incredible woman and don't ever forget that. Thank you for your friendship.

Gorgeous Amy, you have always stood by me in all that I have done, and are my vault! Thank you.

To Ali V, you were always there for me, guiding me and are a sincere friend. I first shared the beautiful side of death with you and Nicc and your belief in me propelled me forward. Thank you.

To my beautiful friend Stacey, I remember those days drawing up the first drafts of my business ideas. You have been there from the first day and always supported me as a wonderful friend. I am so grateful for you.

Sam Cawthorn, you were the first person I publicly

shared the idea of this book to. Your belief in me was all I needed. Thank you for what you have done for me, and in showing me the way to powerfully share this message with the world as a thought leader and professional speaker. Proximity is Power!

To Jodie Spiteri-James and all of the coaches and staff at Speakers Institute, I have loved my journey and you were all an influential part in helping me to launch my speaking career with the world.

Thank you to the Speakers Institute graduates whom I met and formed wonderful friendships with including Ha-Le Thai, Heather Gonzalez, Rita Barbagallo, Heather Joy Bassett and Eve Broenland. There was a reason we all met and you are an important part of my life. Thank you also to Speakers Tribe SA – I love what we are creating in South Australia for professional speaking.

To Shar Moore, YMag was the vehicle I chose to launch *The Love in Death* movement in Australia and in turn the world. What you have created is extraordinary for entrepreneurial women. Thank you for coming into my life. I feel confident that as my mentor and friend, the next steps will be just as exciting.

Thank you, Jennifer Sharp from Daisy Lane Publishing. We crossed paths at the perfect time, you have been instrumental in bringing this book to life.

Thank you, Anne Lucas from Chapter Four Marketing for your friendship, and all you have done to date with this book and *The Love in Death* movement. I am so grateful for your support.

Thank you, Mel Pepers from Bonbo for your expertise. From the moment we spoke, you just got what I am creating, and you bring this to life through graphics, every time, including this book cover. You are amazing.

To Haley Renee from Haley Renee Photography, you are extraordinary. Thank you for capturing the perfect shots. Your work is outstanding.

Thank you, to everyone who has ever believed in me, supported me and encouraged me in everything that I have done throughout my life. I am so grateful for you all.

A heartfelt thank you to my Mum and Dad, for giving me life, and showing me what freedom meant growing up in the country. I have never forgotten that feeling of total freedom to be anything I want to be.

And lastly, an acknowledgement to me, for never giving up, despite the many obstacles. For having the courage to step into something new, and to trust my instinct. To know when I was on purpose, and to keep believing in myself, despite some dream stealers. I ignored the gossip, the bullies, and the hurtful words. I likened myself to a *graceful warrior* who stood tall, and kept believing in herself. I knew in my heart what I was put on this earth to do. I knew in my heart how I can make a fundamental difference and to aid in people's healing. I trusted in myself. I believed. And for that, I am so happy, fulfilled and grateful.

Sharon Muscet

About the author

Sharon Muscet is one of Australia's foremost experts on healing and loss. As one of the country's most sought-after celebrants, Sharon has worked alongside thousands of

individuals experiencing the realities of death; giving her privileged insight into not only how to cope with grief and loss but, more importantly, the life lessons learned from those who pass.

A life-threatening accident and near-death experience led Sharon to walk away from a successful international corporate career in PR & Marketing. Her journey as a celebrant began after a friend asked her to speak at her Father's funeral and, from that moment, Sharon's life would change forever.

Since 2011, Sharon has conducted several hundred *Celebrations of Life* for families grieving the loss of a loved one and speaks about death to approximately one thousand people per week.

Today, Sharon is also called upon as a celebrated international keynote speaker to share powerful stories, life lessons and love stories from those who have passed with a view of helping others to live their best life. As the Founder of *The Love in Death* movement, Sharon is changing the conversation that comes with death from one of fear to one of love. Inspiring audiences all over the world to reflect on their own life, transform them to take-action and change not only the way they die but the way in which they live their life.

Sharon has been named YMag's *2019 Female Thought Leader* and in September 2019 won YMag's *The Disruptor Award* for leading a global movement that is changing lives.

She is the mother of two incredible boys and resides in Adelaide, Australia.

www.ingramcontent.com/pod-product-compliance
Lightning Source LLC
Chambersburg PA
CBHW071909290426
44110CB00013B/1334